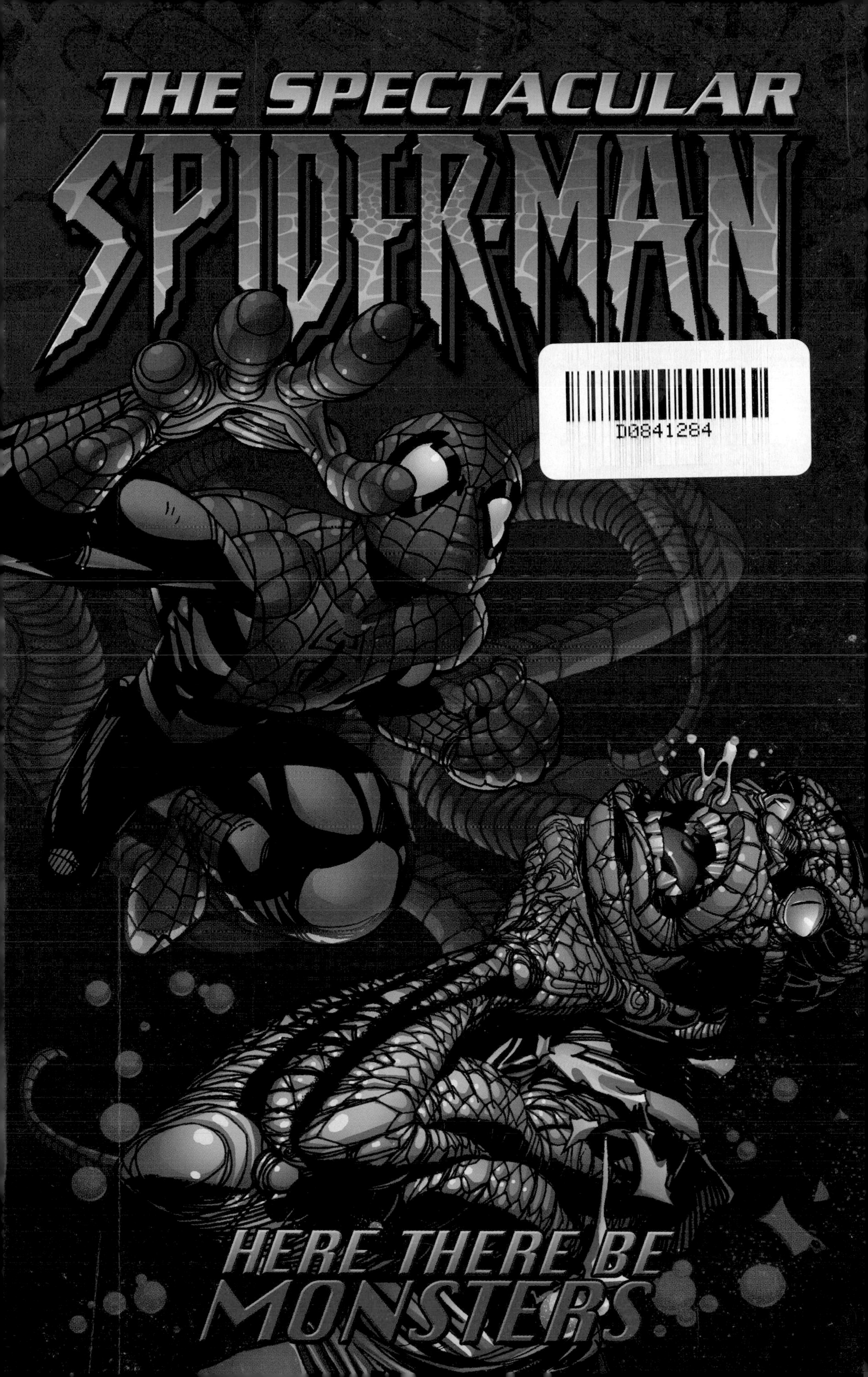
THE SPECTACULAR
SPIDER-MAN
HERE THERE BE
MONSTERS

THE SPECTACULAR SPIDER-MAN

HERE THERE BE MONSTERS

Writer: Paul Jenkins

Art, Issues #11-13
Penciler: Damion Scott
Inker: Rob Campanella
Colorist: Frank D'Armata & Studio F's Edgar Delgado

Art, Issue #14
Painter: Paolo Rivera

Letterer: Virtual Calligraphy's Cory Petit
Cover Art: Paolo Rivera
Assistant Editors: Andy Schmidt & Nicole Wiley
Editors: John Miesegaes, Axel Alonso & Tom Brevoort

Collections Editor: Jeff Youngquist
Assistant Editor: Jennifer Grünwald

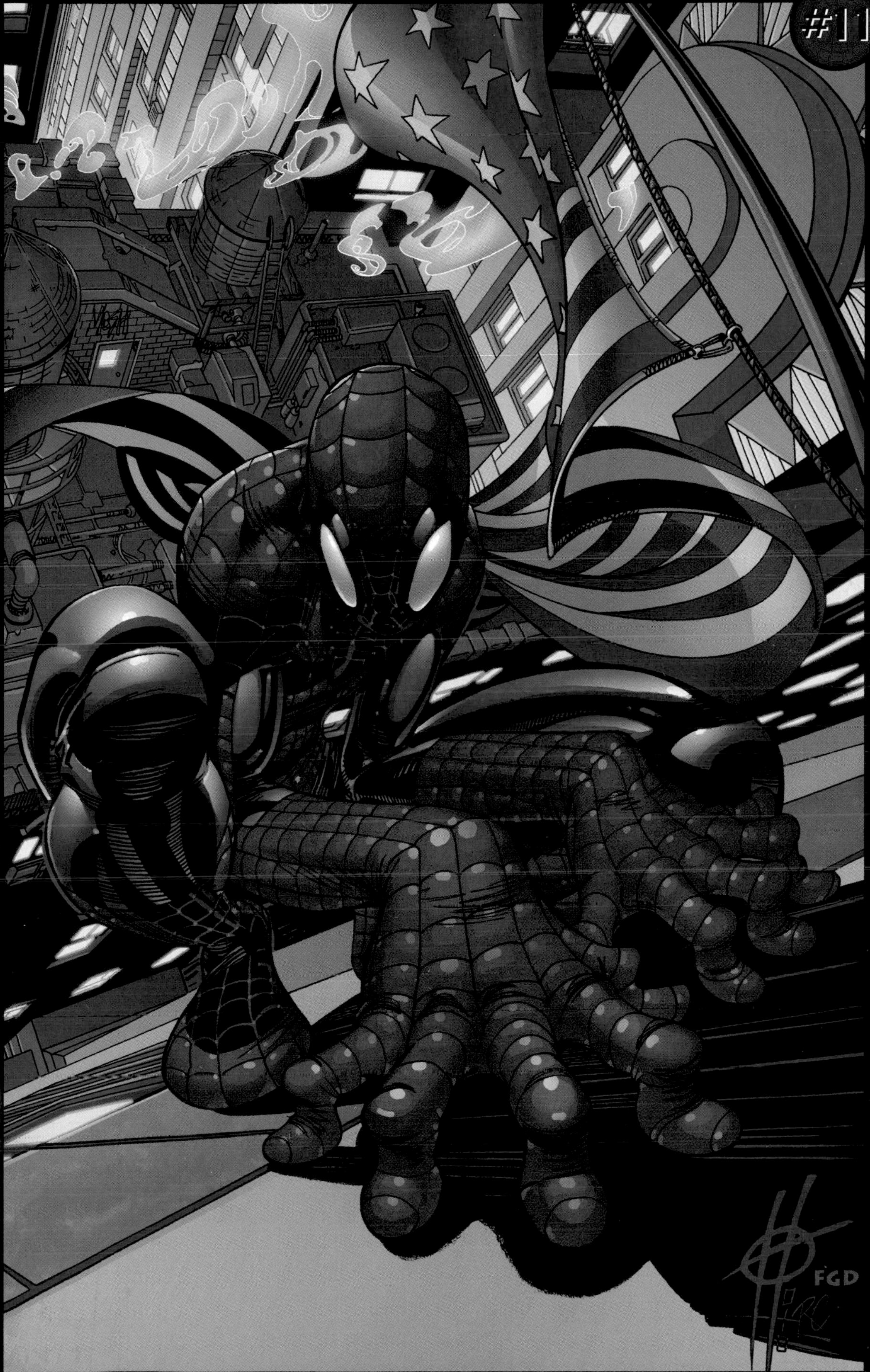
#11
FGD

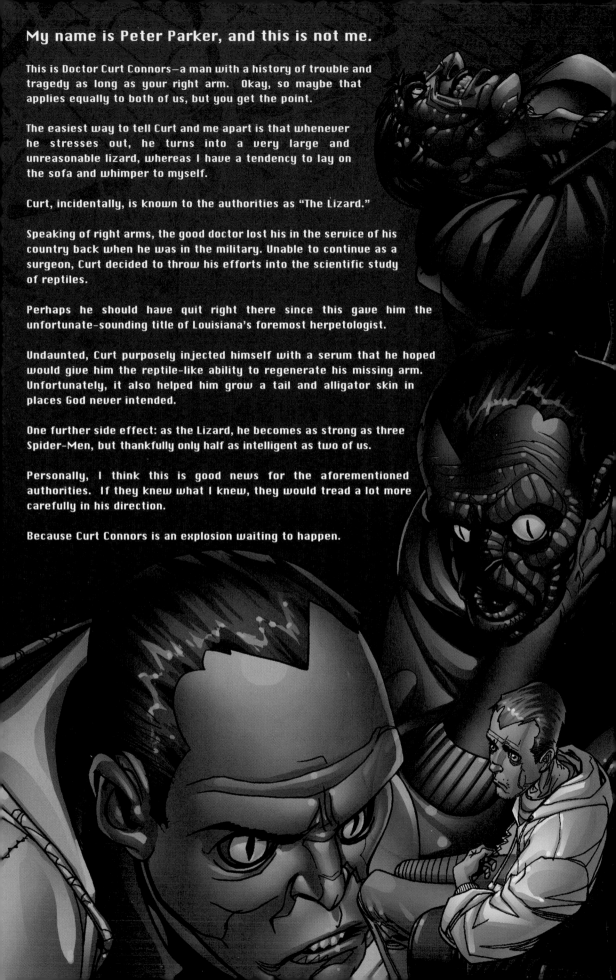

My name is Peter Parker, and this is not me.

This is Doctor Curt Connors—a man with a history of trouble and tragedy as long as your right arm. Okay, so maybe that applies equally to both of us, but you get the point.

The easiest way to tell Curt and me apart is that whenever he stresses out, he turns into a very large and unreasonable lizard, whereas I have a tendency to lay on the sofa and whimper to myself.

Curt, incidentally, is known to the authorities as "The Lizard."

Speaking of right arms, the good doctor lost his in the service of his country back when he was in the military. Unable to continue as a surgeon, Curt decided to throw his efforts into the scientific study of reptiles.

Perhaps he should have quit right there since this gave him the unfortunate-sounding title of Louisiana's foremost herpetologist.

Undaunted, Curt purposely injected himself with a serum that he hoped would give him the reptile-like ability to regenerate his missing arm. Unfortunately, it also helped him grow a tail and alligator skin in places God never intended.

One further side effect: as the Lizard, he becomes as strong as three Spider-Men, but thankfully only half as intelligent as two of us.

Personally, I think this is good news for the aforementioned authorities. If they knew what I knew, they would tread a lot more carefully in his direction.

Because Curt Connors is an explosion waiting to happen.

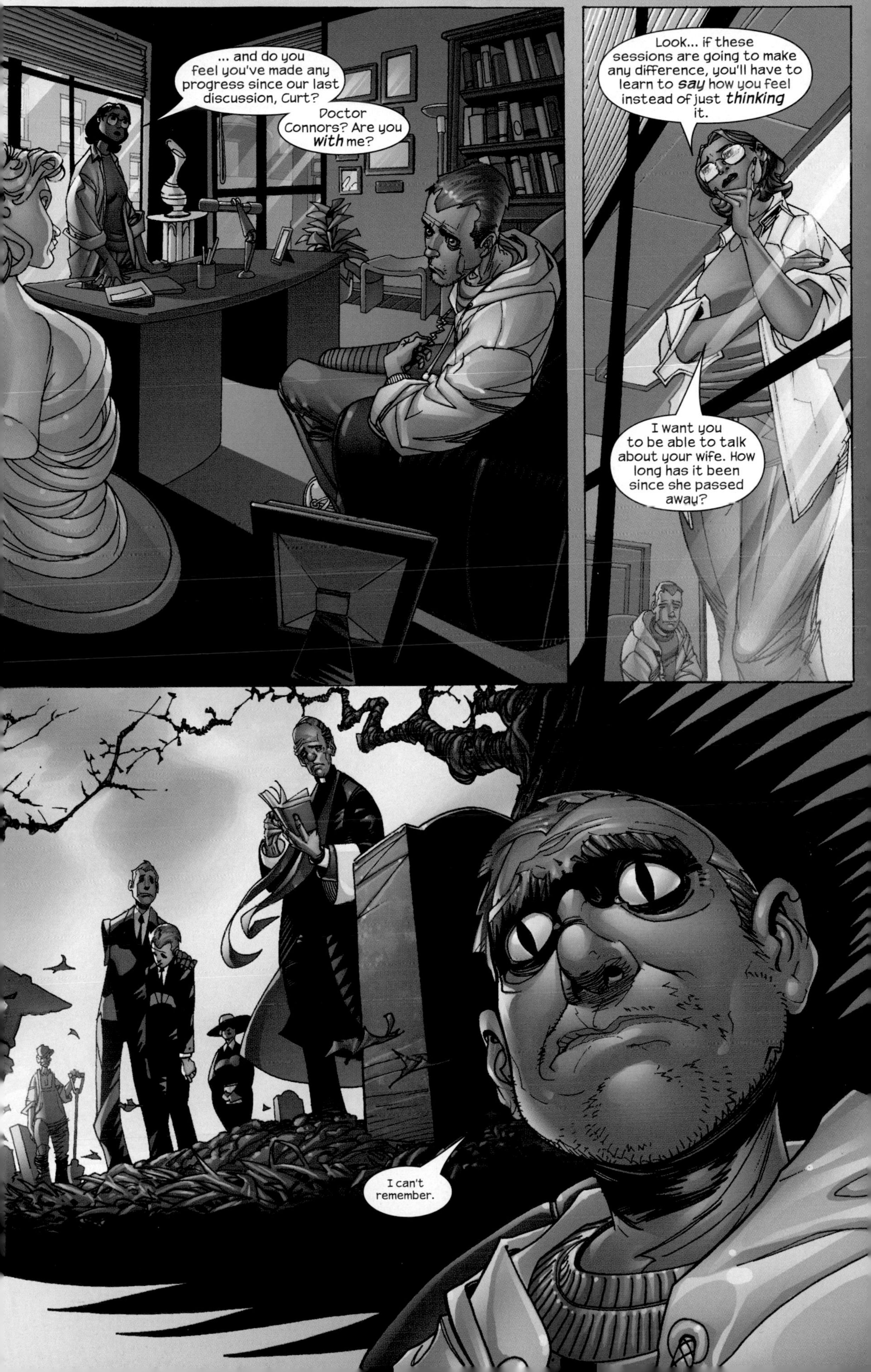
... and do you feel you've made any progress since our last discussion, Curt?
Doctor Connors? Are you *with* me?
Look... if these sessions are going to make any difference, you'll have to learn to *say* how you feel instead of just *thinking* it.
I want you to be able to talk about your wife. How long has it been since she passed away?
I can't remember.

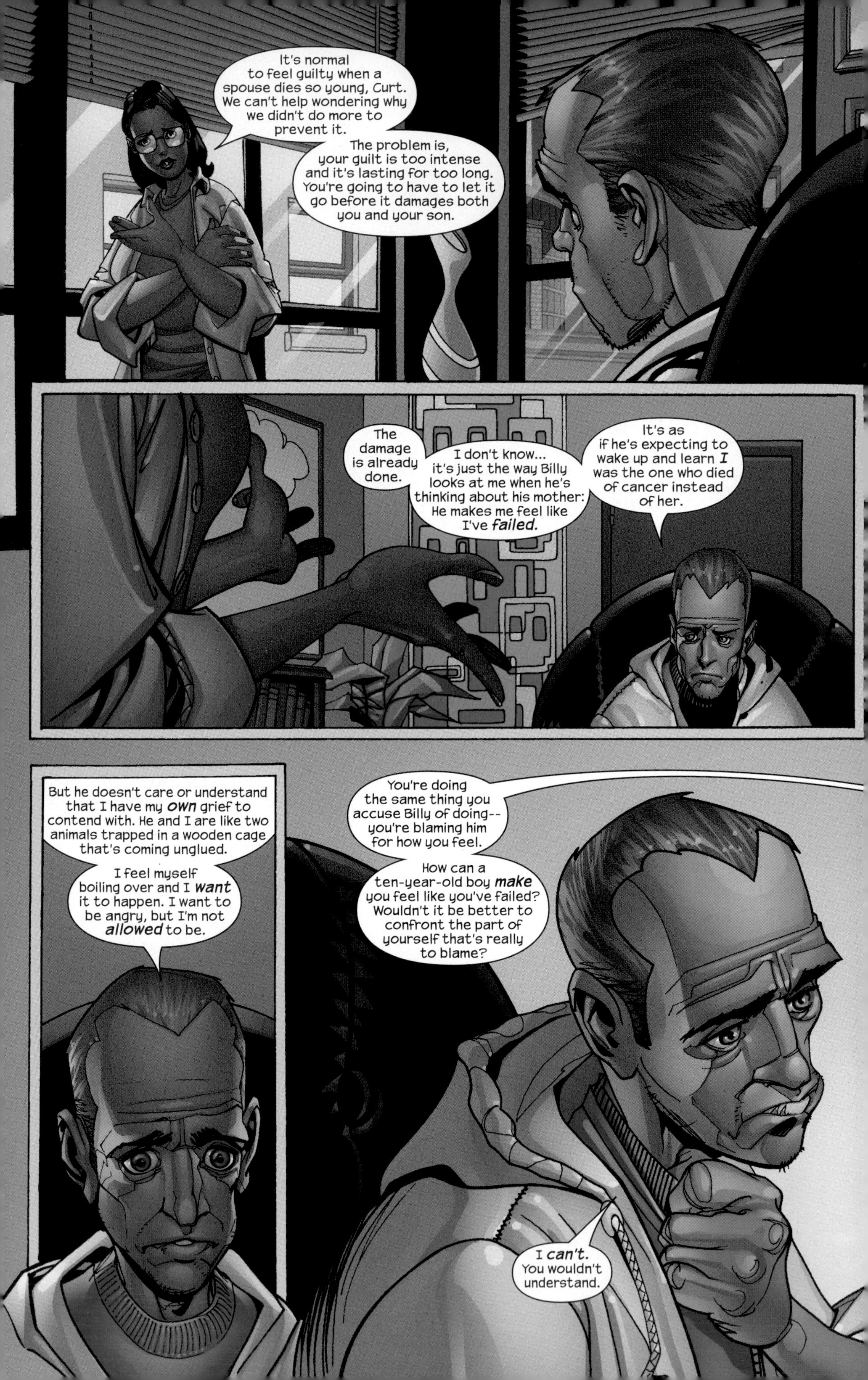

It's normal to feel guilty when a spouse dies so young, Curt. We can't help wondering why we didn't do more to prevent it.
The problem is, your guilt is too intense and it's lasting for too long. You're going to have to let it go before it damages both you and your son.
The damage is already done.
I don't know... it's just the way Billy looks at me when he's thinking about his mother: He makes me feel like I've *failed.*
It's as if he's expecting to wake up and learn *I* was the one who died of cancer instead of her.
But he doesn't care or understand that I have my *own* grief to contend with. He and I are like two animals trapped in a wooden cage that's coming unglued.
I feel myself boiling over and I *want* it to happen. I want to be angry, but I'm not *allowed* to be.
You're doing the same thing you accuse Billy of doing-- you're blaming him for how you feel.
How can a ten-year-old boy *make* you feel like you've failed? Wouldn't it be better to confront the part of yourself that's really to blame?
I *can't.* You wouldn't understand.

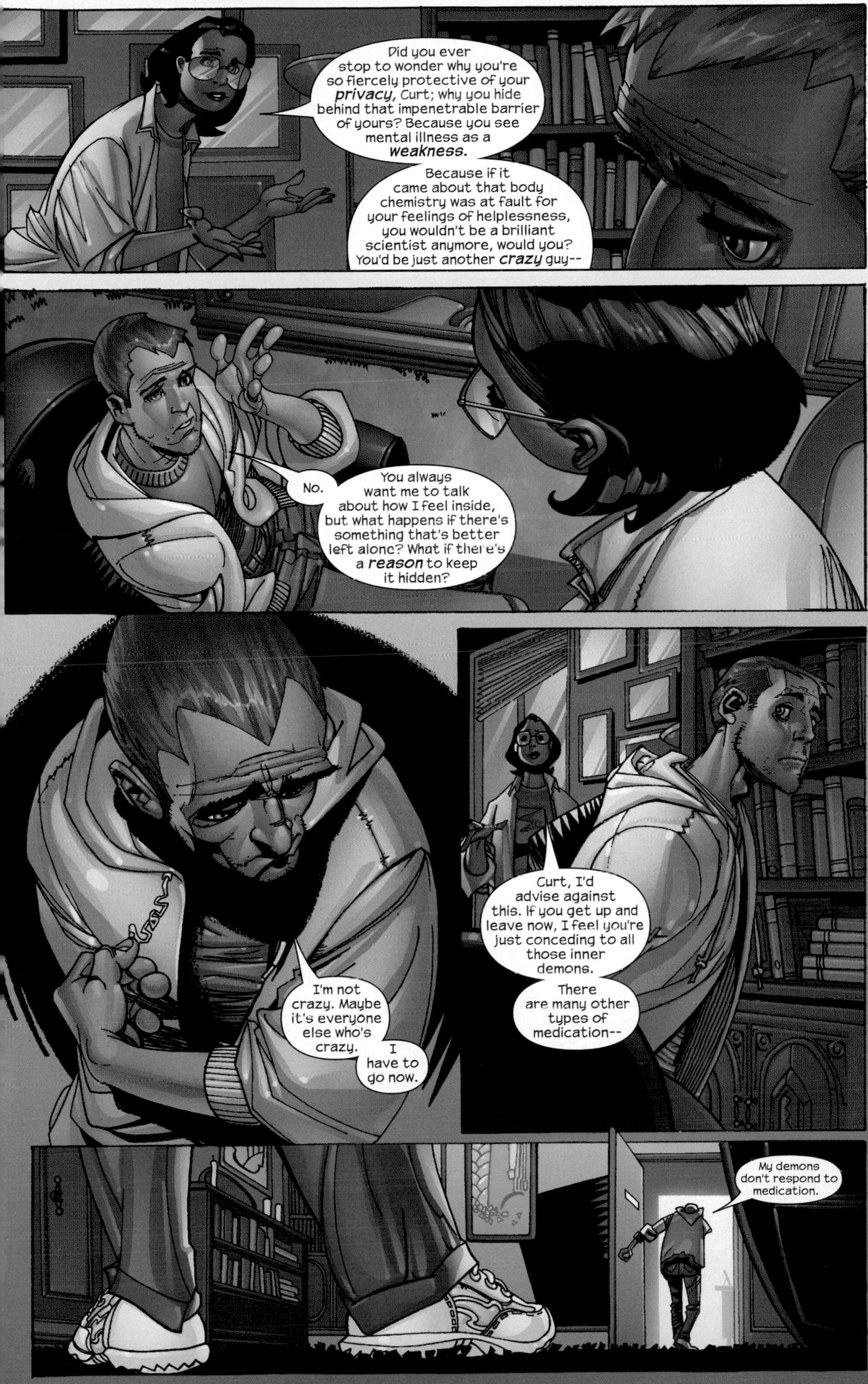
Did you ever stop to wonder why you're so fiercely protective of your *privacy*, Curt; why you hide behind that impenetrable barrier of yours? Because you see mental illness as a *weakness.*
Because if it came about that body chemistry was at fault for your feelings of helplessness, you wouldn't be a brilliant scientist anymore, would you? You'd be just another *crazy* guy--
No.
You always want me to talk about how I feel inside, but what happens if there's something that's better left alone? What if there's a *reason* to keep it hidden?
I'm not crazy. Maybe it's everyone else who's crazy.
I have to go now.
Curt, I'd advise against this. If you get up and leave now, I feel you're just conceding to all those inner demons.
There are many other types of medication--
My demons don't respond to medication.

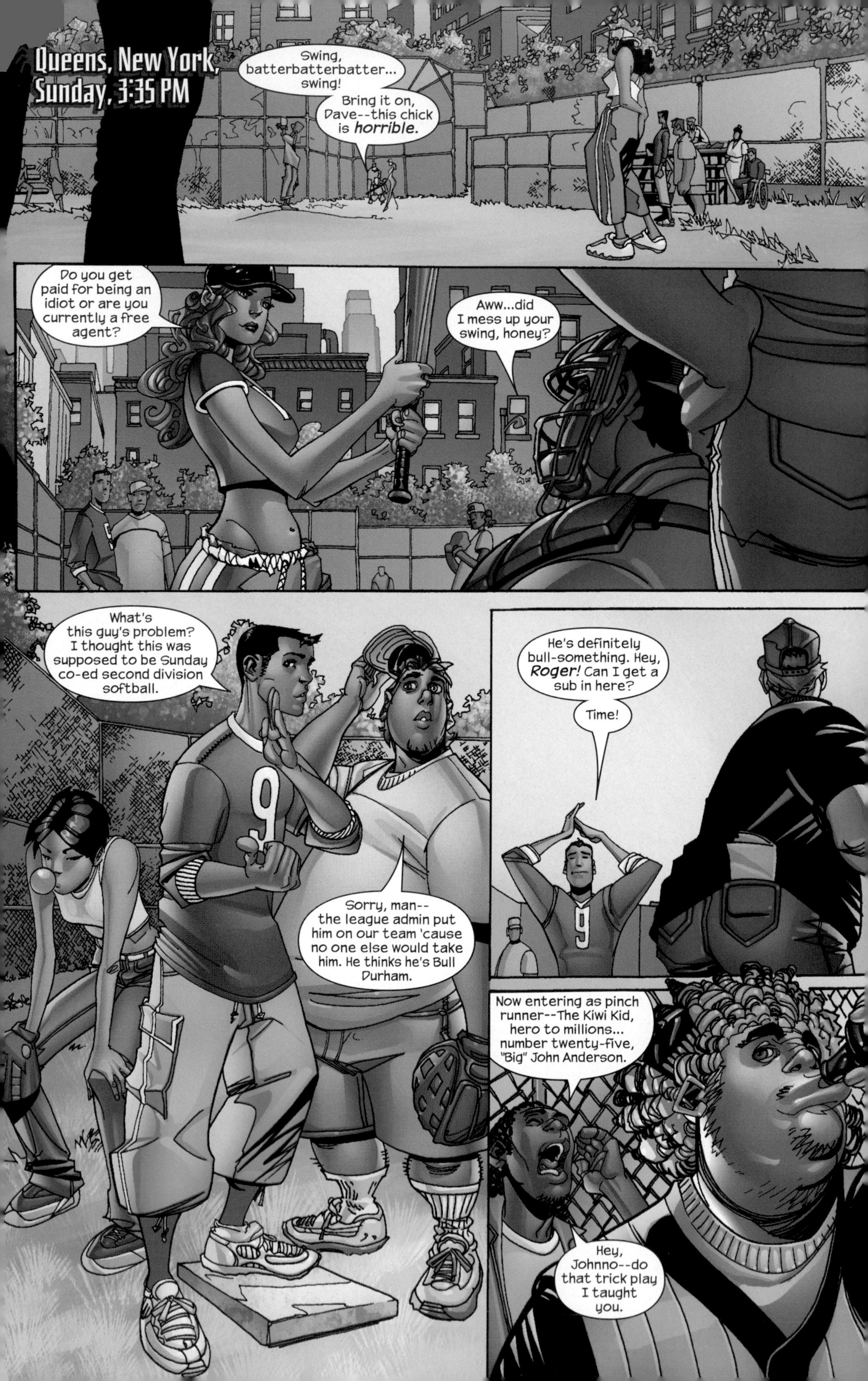
Queens, New York, Sunday, 3:35 PM
Swing, batterbatterbatter... swing!
Bring it on, Dave--this chick is *horrible.*
Do you get paid for being an idiot or are you currently a free agent?
Aww...did I mess up your swing, honey?
What's this guy's problem? I thought this was supposed to be Sunday co-ed second division softball.
Sorry, man-- the league admin put him on our team 'cause no one else would take him. He thinks he's Bull Durham.
He's definitely bull-something. Hey, *Roger!* Can I get a sub in here?
Time!
Now entering as pinch runner--The Kiwi Kid, hero to millions... number twenty-five, "Big" John Anderson.
Hey, Johnno--do that trick play I taught you.

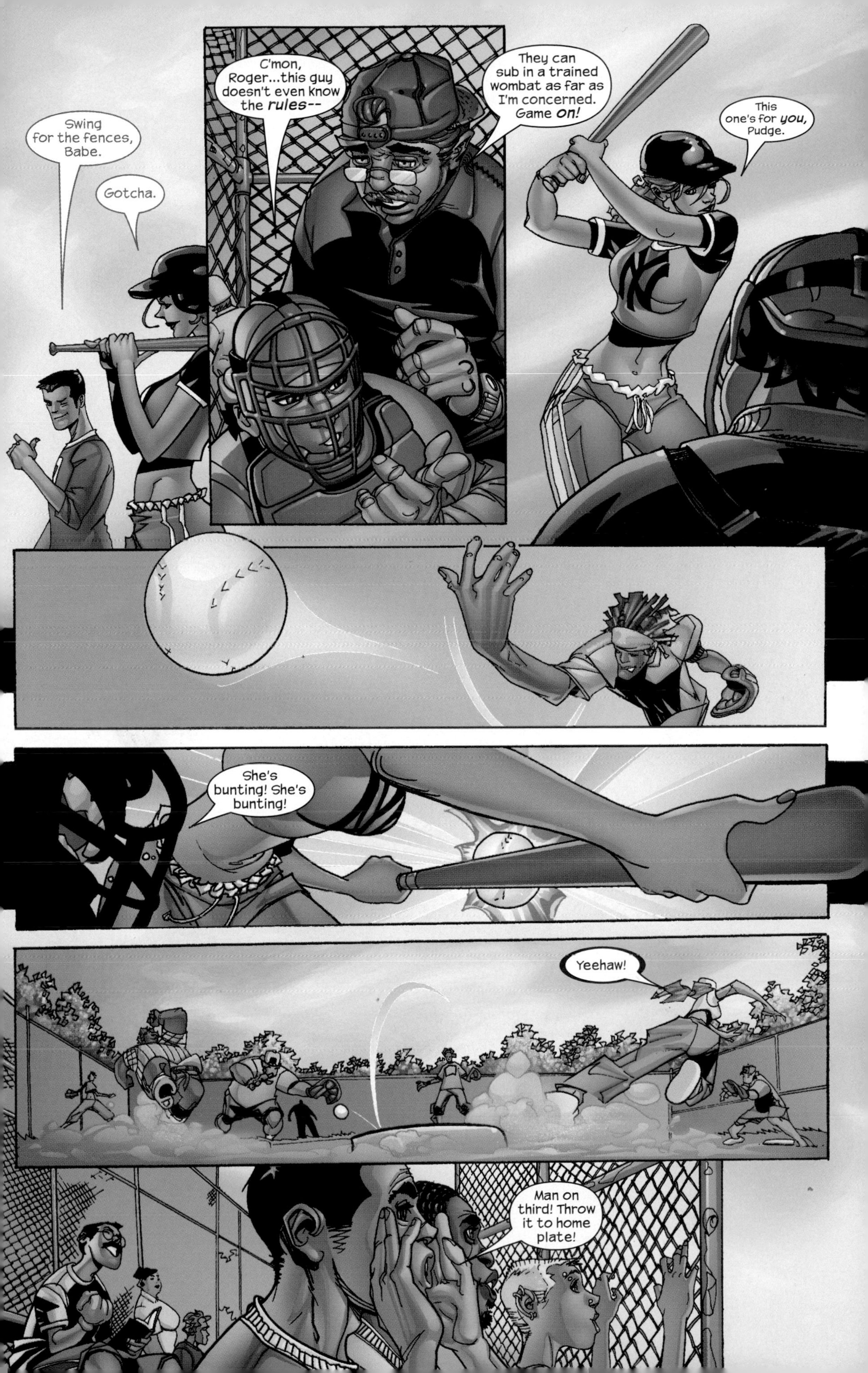
Swing for the fences, Babe.
Gotcha.
C'mon, Roger...this guy doesn't even know the *rules*--
They can sub in a trained wombat as far as I'm concerned. Game *on!*
This one's for *you,* Pudge.
She's bunting! She's bunting!
Yeehaw!
Man on third! Throw it to home plate!

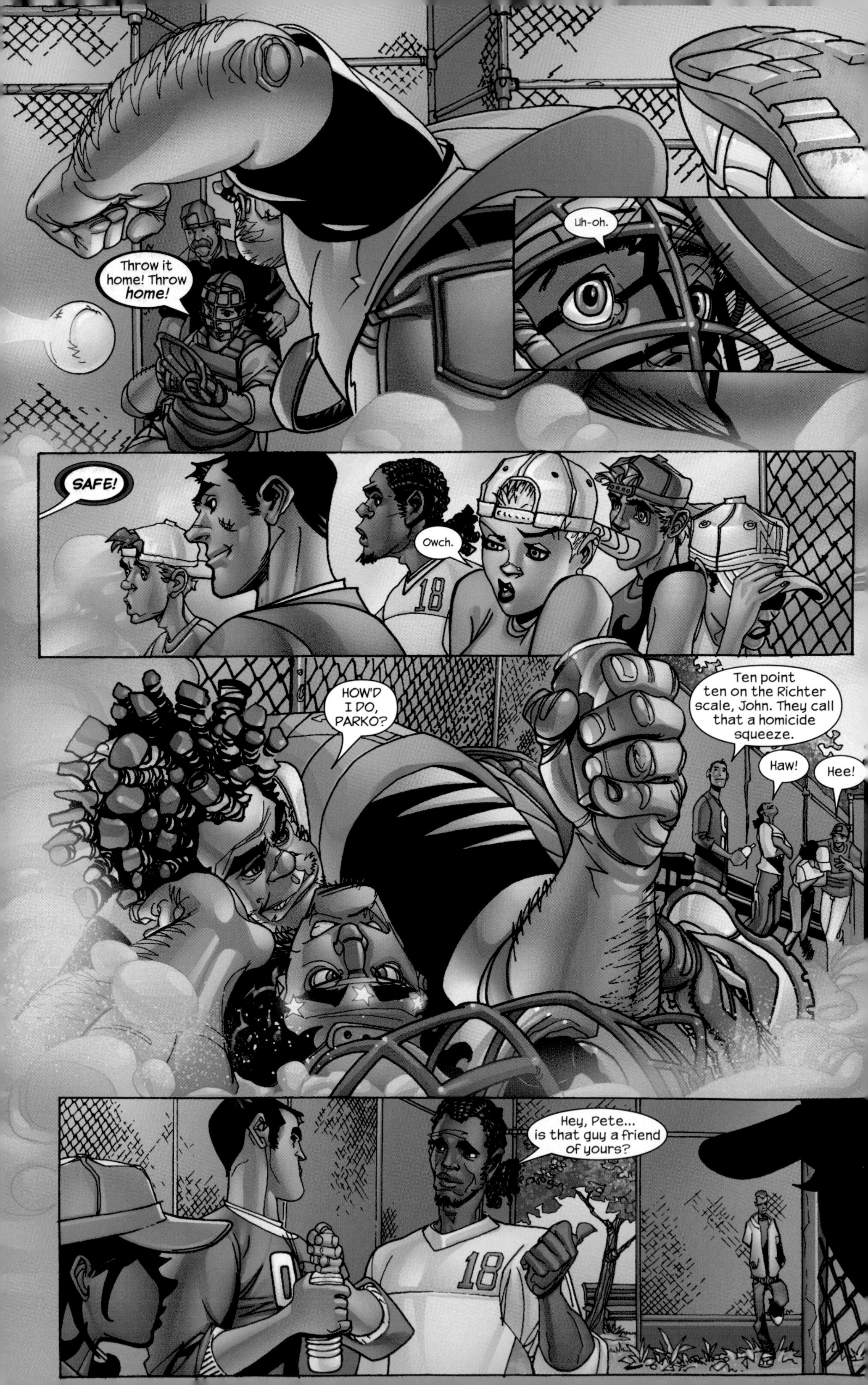
Throw it home! Throw *home!*
Uh-oh.
SAFE!
Owch.
HOW'D I DO, PARKO?
Ten point ten on the Richter scale, John. They call that a homicide squeeze.
Haw!
Hee!
Hey, Pete... is that guy a friend of yours?

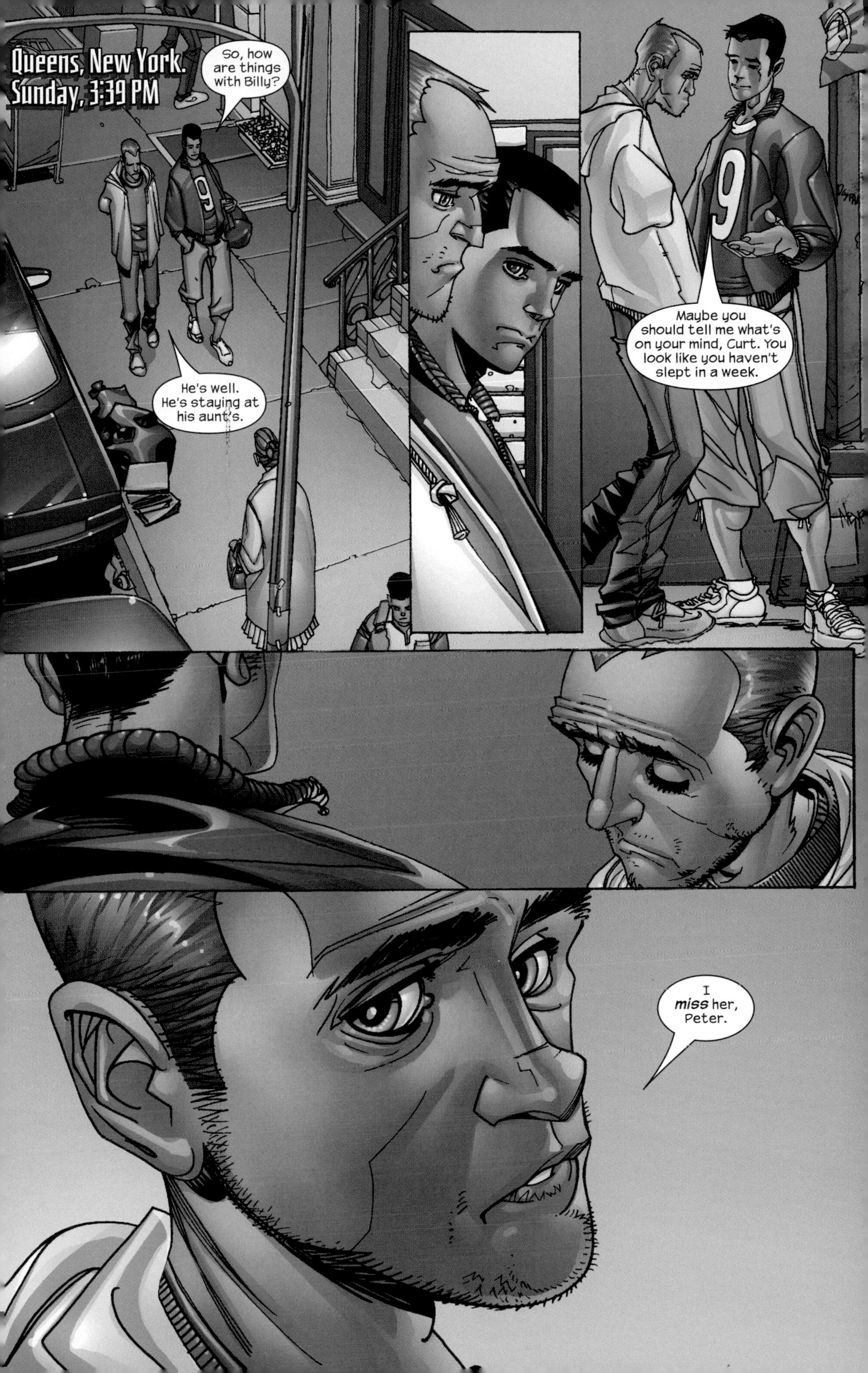
Queens, New York.
Sunday, 3:39 PM
So, how are things with Billy?
He's well. He's staying at his aunt's.
Maybe you should tell me what's on your mind, Curt. You look like you haven't slept in a week.
I *miss* her, Peter.

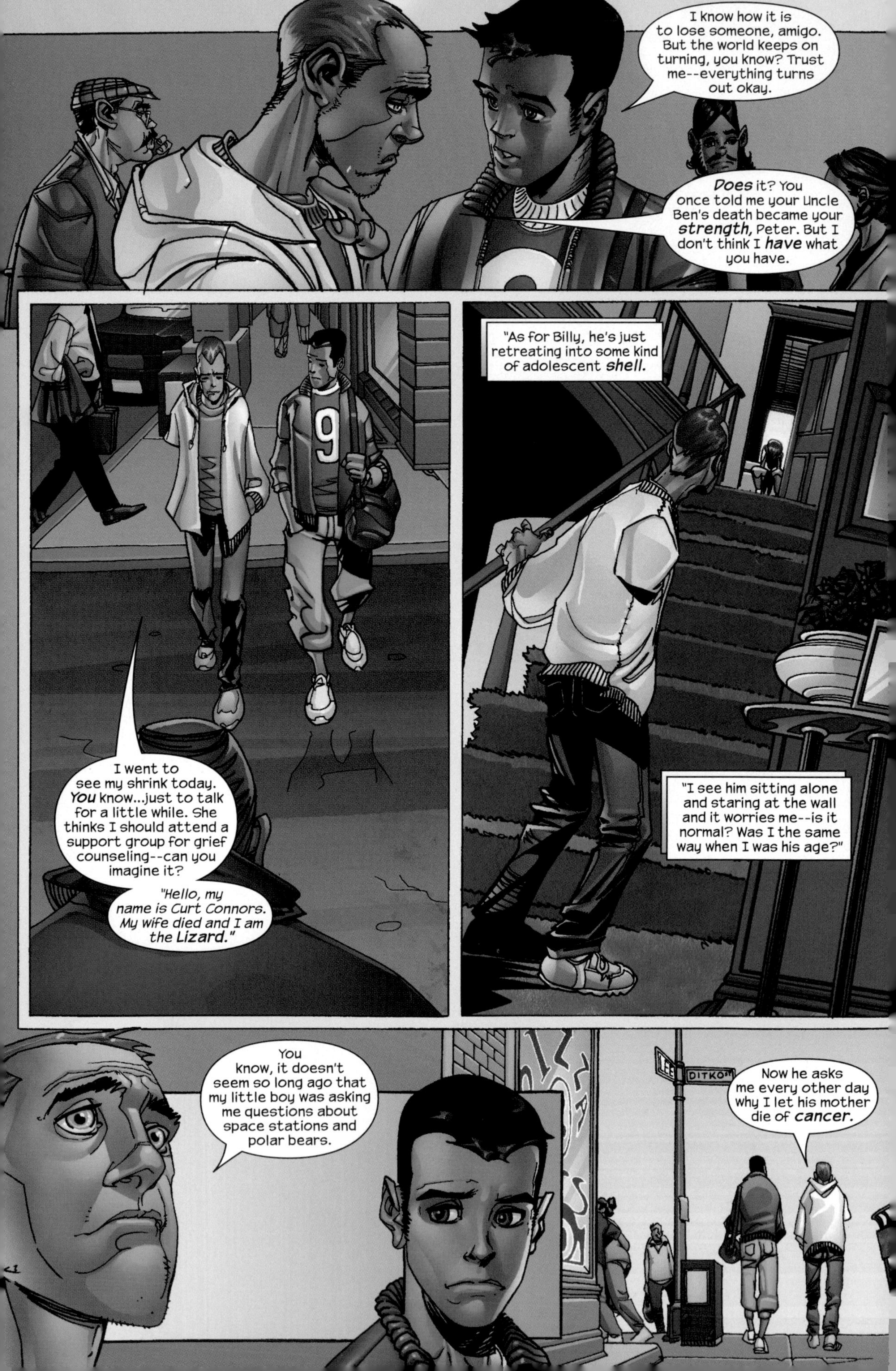
I know how it is to lose someone, amigo. But the world keeps on turning, you know? Trust me--everything turns out okay.
Does it? You once told me your Uncle Ben's death became your strength, Peter. But I don't think I have what you have.
I went to see my shrink today. You know...just to talk for a little while. She thinks I should attend a support group for grief counseling--can you imagine it?
"Hello, my name is Curt Connors. My wife died and I am the Lizard."
"As for Billy, he's just retreating into some kind of adolescent shell.
"I see him sitting alone and staring at the wall and it worries me--is it normal? Was I the same way when I was his age?"
You know, it doesn't seem so long ago that my little boy was asking me questions about space stations and polar bears.
LEE
DITKO
Now he asks me every other day why I let his mother die of cancer.

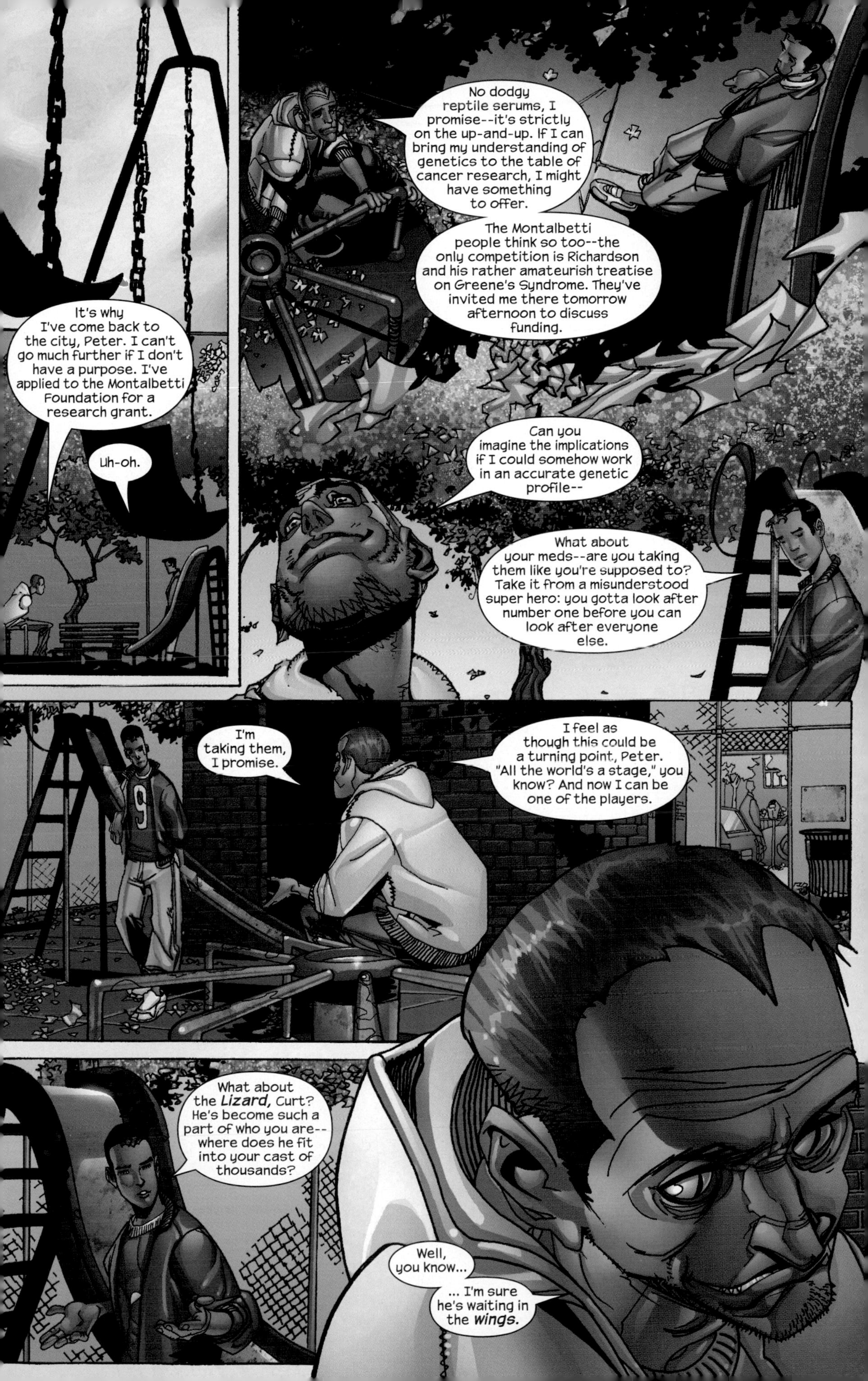

It's why I've come back to the city, Peter. I can't go much further if I don't have a purpose. I've applied to the Montalbetti Foundation for a research grant.
Uh-oh.
No dodgy reptile serums, I promise--it's strictly on the up-and-up. If I can bring my understanding of genetics to the table of cancer research, I might have something to offer.
The Montalbetti people think so too--the only competition is Richardson and his rather amateurish treatise on Greene's Syndrome. They've invited me there tomorrow afternoon to discuss funding.
Can you imagine the implications if I could somehow work in an accurate genetic profile--
What about your meds--are you taking them like you're supposed to? Take it from a misunderstood super hero: you gotta look after number one before you can look after everyone else.
I'm taking them, I promise.
I feel as though this could be a turning point, Peter. "All the world's a stage," you know? And now I can be one of the players.
What about the *Lizard,* Curt? He's become such a part of who you are--where does he fit into your cast of thousands?
Well, you know...
... I'm sure he's waiting in the *wings.*

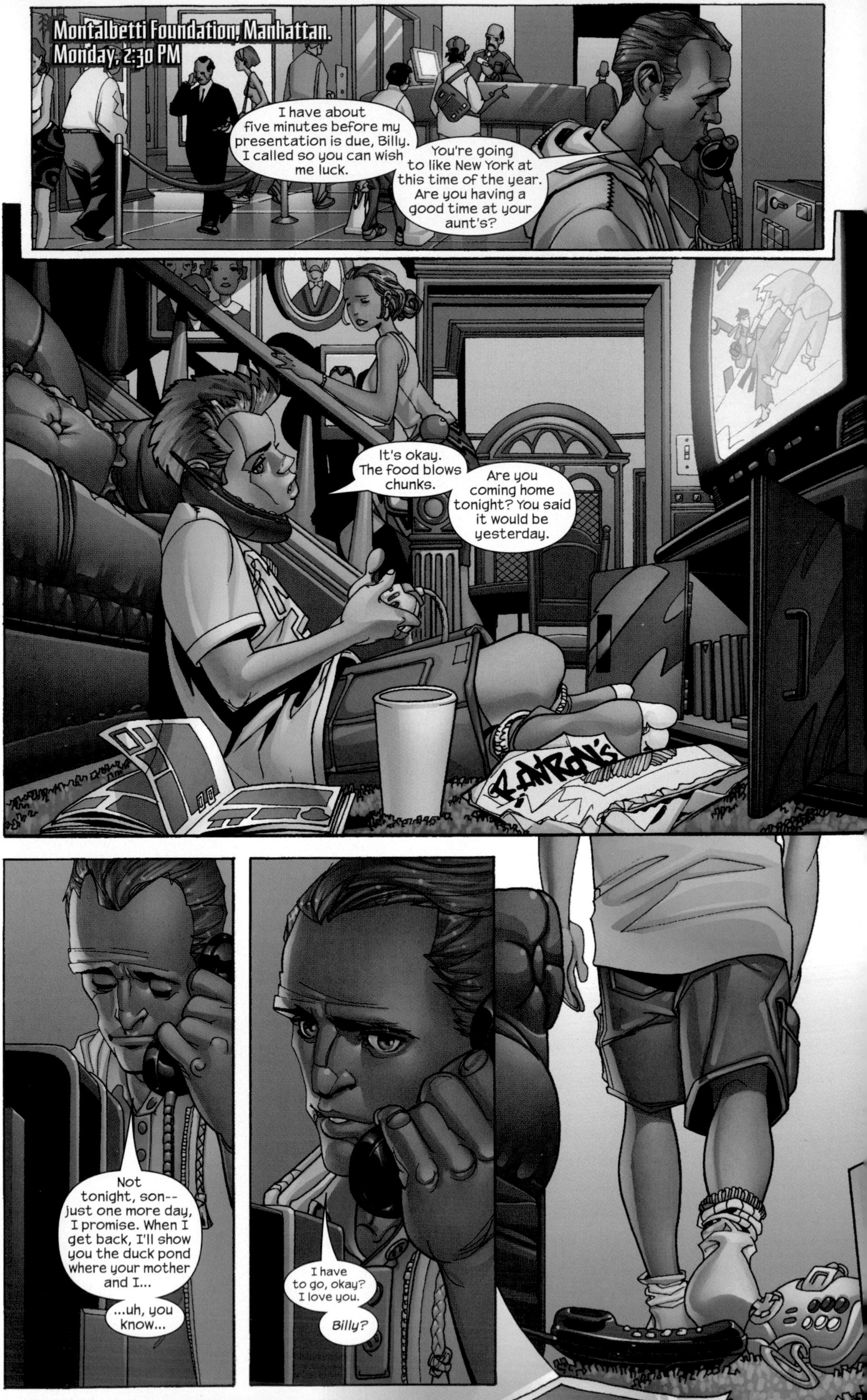

Montalbetti Foundation, Manhattan. Monday, 2:30 PM
I have about five minutes before my presentation is due, Billy. I called so you can wish me luck.
You're going to like New York at this time of the year. Are you having a good time at your aunt's?
It's okay. The food blows chunks.
Are you coming home tonight? You said it would be yesterday.
Not tonight, son-- just one more day, I promise. When I get back, I'll show you the duck pond where your mother and I...
...uh, you know...
I have to go, okay? I love you.
Billy?

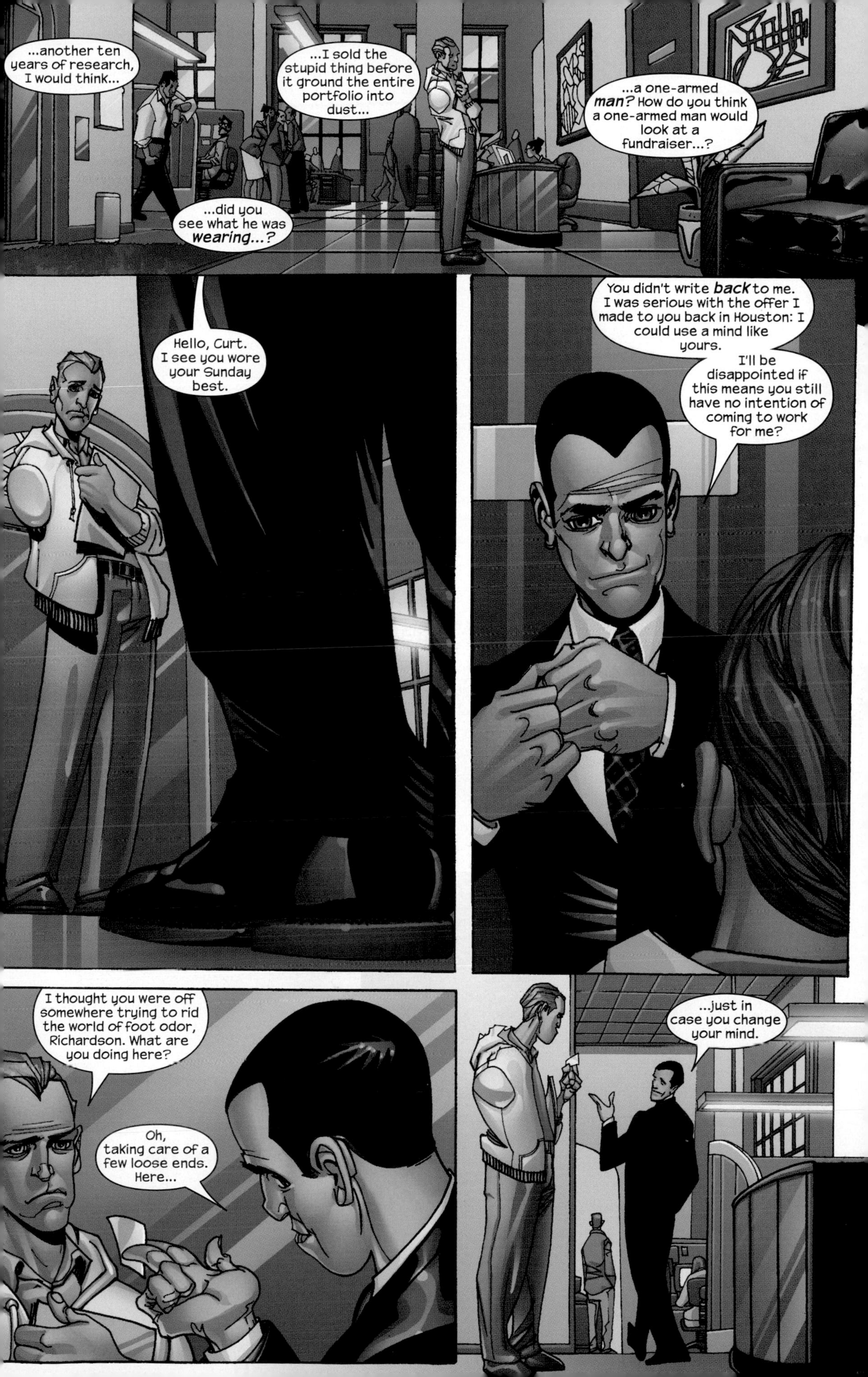

...another ten years of research, I would think...
...I sold the stupid thing before it ground the entire portfolio into dust...
...a one-armed *man?* How do you think a one-armed man would look at a fundraiser...?
...did you see what he was *wearing...?*
Hello, Curt. I see you wore your Sunday best.
You didn't write *back* to me. I was serious with the offer I made to you back in Houston: I could use a mind like yours.
I'll be disappointed if this means you still have no intention of coming to work for me?
I thought you were off somewhere trying to rid the world of foot odor, Richardson. What are you doing here?
Oh, taking care of a few loose ends. Here...
...just in case you change your mind.

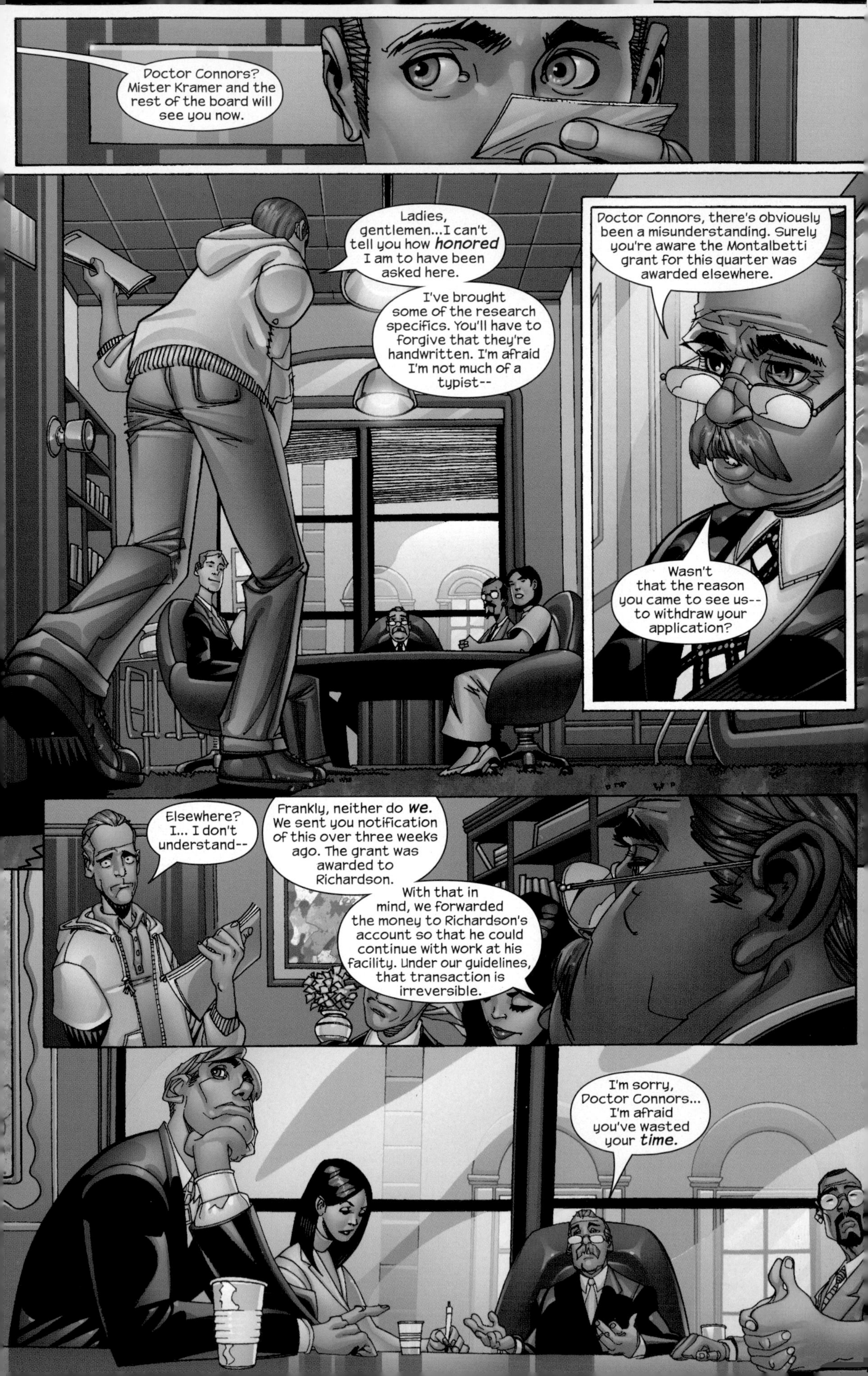

Doctor Connors? Mister Kramer and the rest of the board will see you now.
Ladies, gentlemen...I can't tell you how *honored* I am to have been asked here.
I've brought some of the research specifics. You'll have to forgive that they're handwritten. I'm afraid I'm not much of a typist--
Doctor Connors, there's obviously been a misunderstanding. Surely you're aware the Montalbetti grant for this quarter was awarded elsewhere.
Wasn't that the reason you came to see us-- to withdraw your application?
Elsewhere? I... I don't understand--
Frankly, neither do *we.* We sent you notification of this over three weeks ago. The grant was awarded to Richardson.
With that in mind, we forwarded the money to Richardson's account so that he could continue with work at his facility. Under our guidelines, that transaction is irreversible.
I'm sorry, Doctor Connors... I'm afraid you've wasted your *time.*

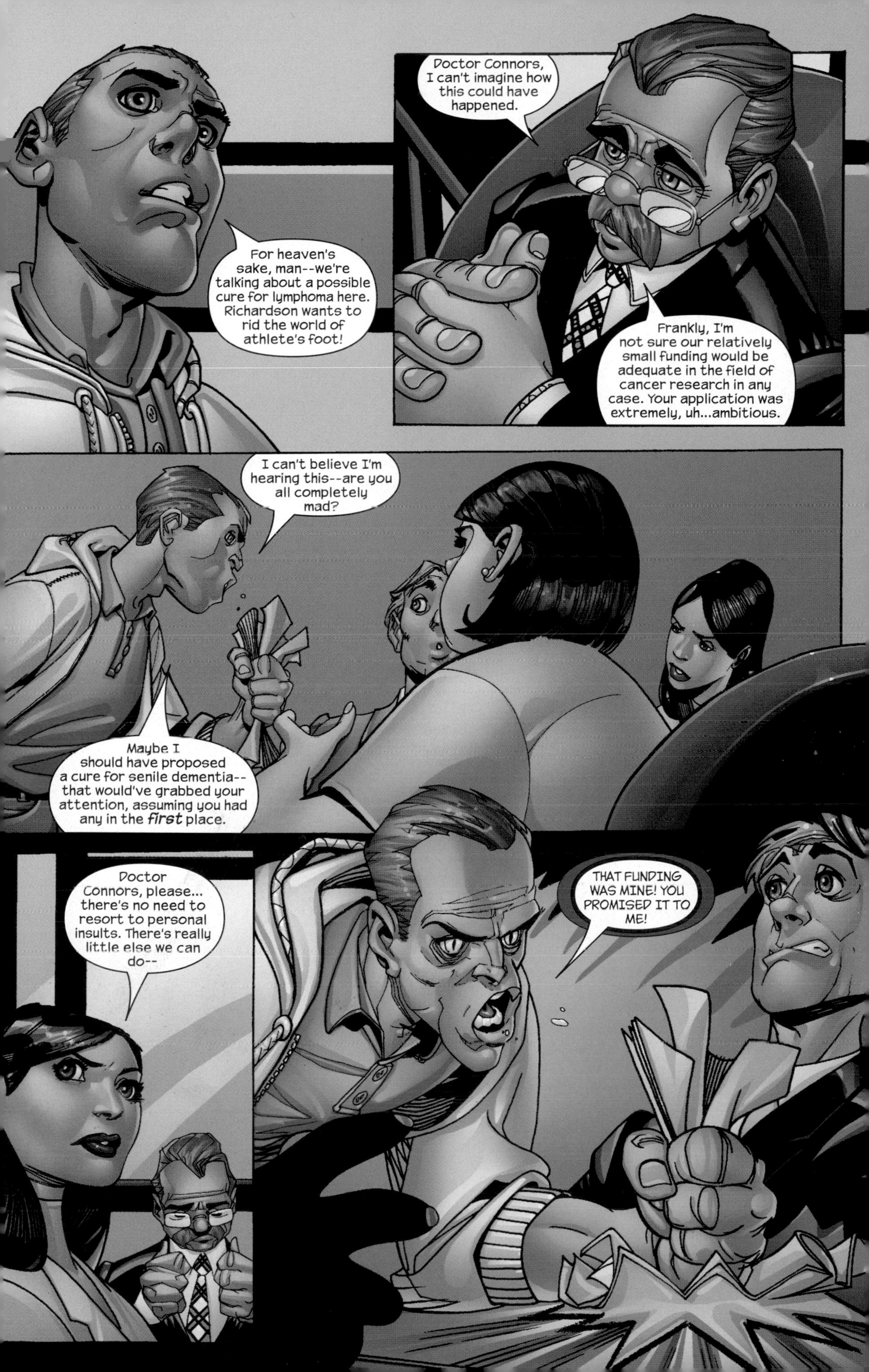
Doctor Connors, I can't imagine how this could have happened.
For heaven's sake, man--we're talking about a possible cure for lymphoma here. Richardson wants to rid the world of athlete's foot!
Frankly, I'm not sure our relatively small funding would be adequate in the field of cancer research in any case. Your application was extremely, uh...ambitious.
I can't believe I'm hearing this--are you all completely mad?
Maybe I should have proposed a cure for senile dementia--that would've grabbed your attention, assuming you had any in the *first* place.
Doctor Connors, please... there's no need to resort to personal insults. There's really little else we can do--
THAT FUNDING WAS MINE! YOU PROMISED IT TO ME!

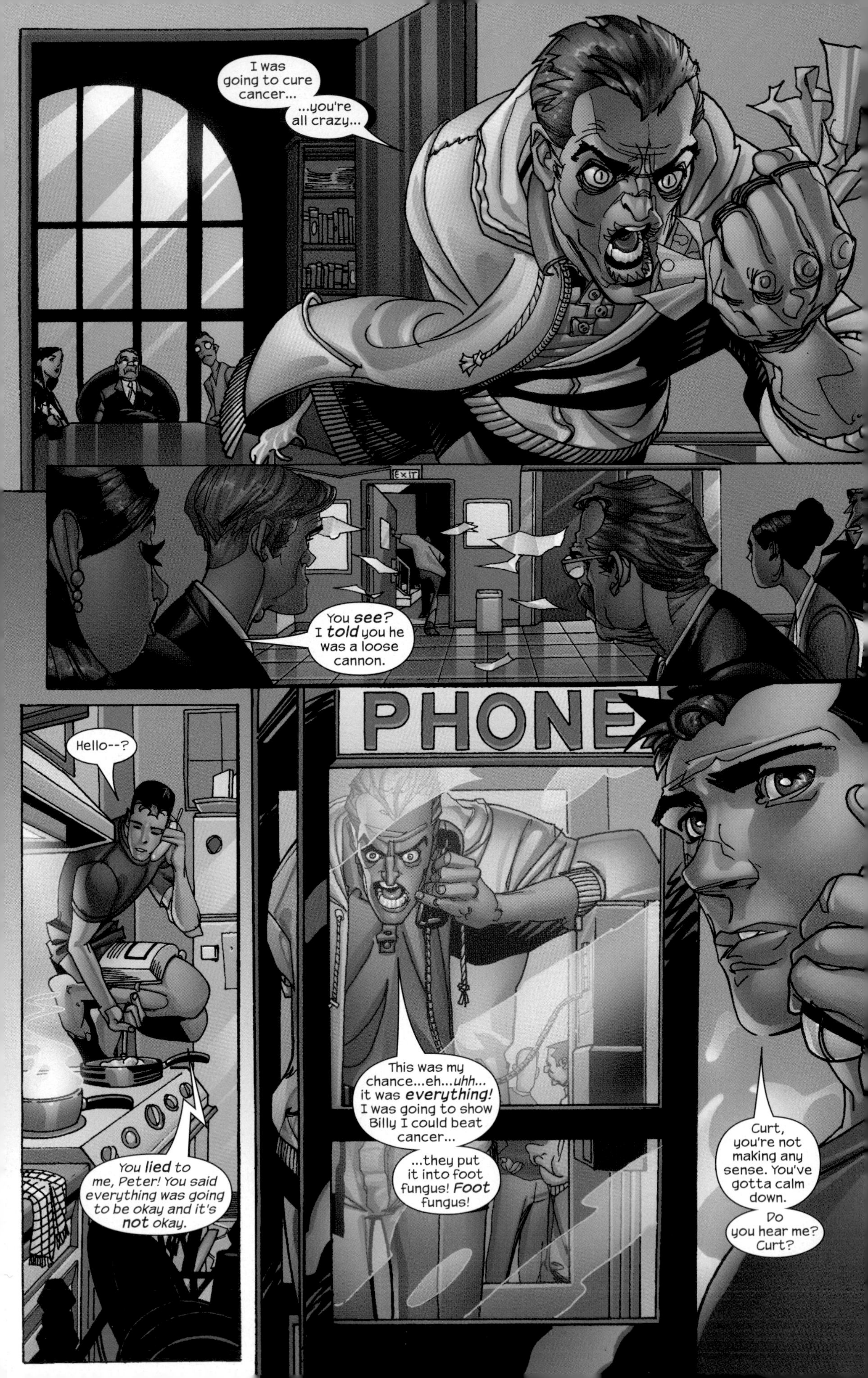
I was going to cure cancer...
...you're all crazy...
You *see?* I *told* you he was a loose cannon.
Hello--?
PHONE
This was my chance...eh...*uhh*... it was *everything!* I was going to show Billy I could beat cancer...
...they put it into foot fungus! *Foot* fungus!
You *lied* to me, Peter! You said everything was going to be okay and it's *not* okay.
Curt, you're not making any sense. You've gotta calm down.
Do you hear me? Curt?

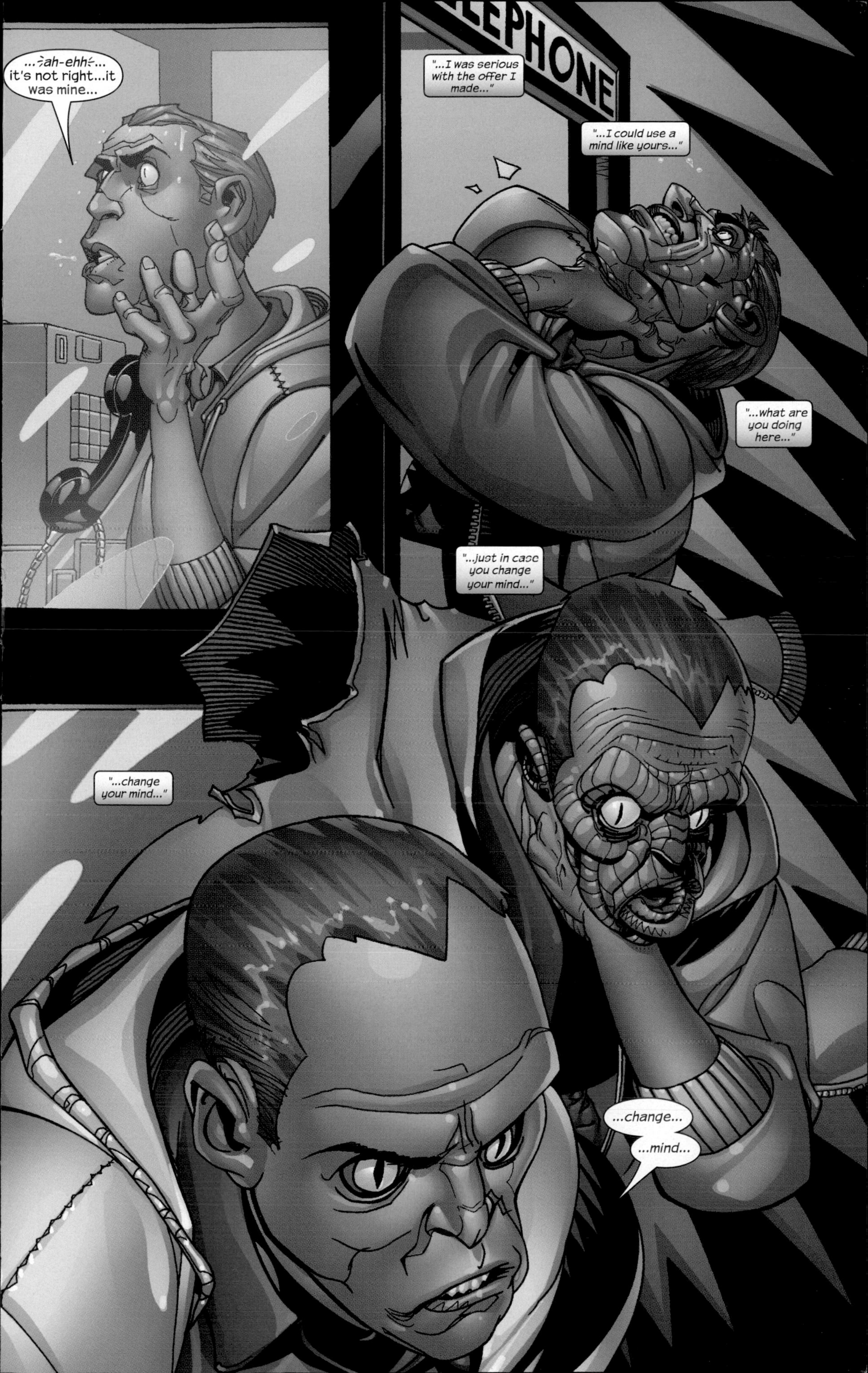
...ah-ehh...
it's not right...it was mine...
"...I was serious with the offer I made..."
"...I could use a mind like yours..."
"...what are you doing here..."
"...just in case you change your mind..."
"...change your mind..."
...change...
...mind...
ELEPHONE

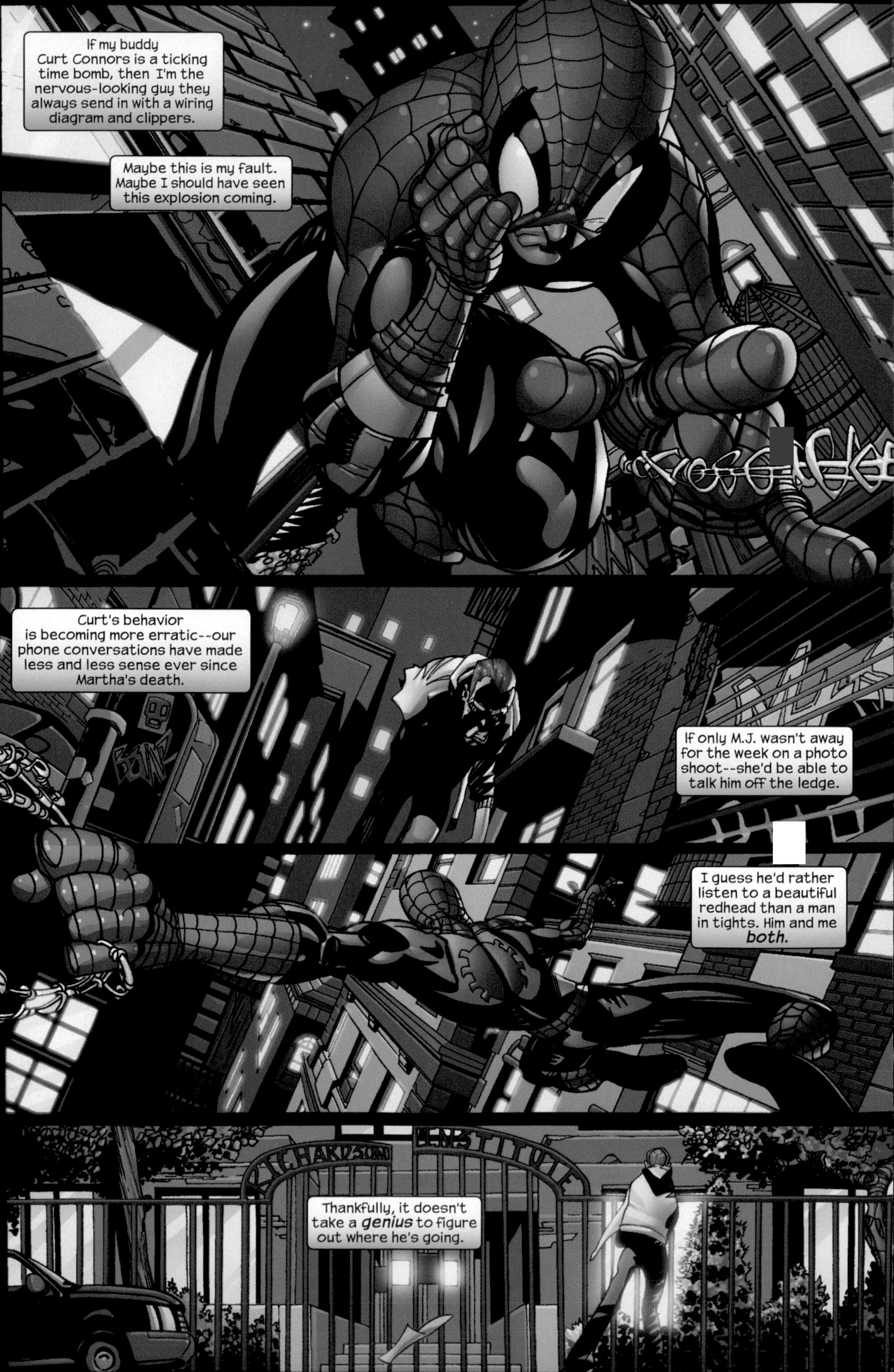

If my buddy Curt Connors is a ticking time bomb, then I'm the nervous-looking guy they always send in with a wiring diagram and clippers.
Maybe this is my fault. Maybe I should have seen this explosion coming.
Curt's behavior is becoming more erratic--our phone conversations have made less and less sense ever since Martha's death.
If only M.J. wasn't away for the week on a photo shoot--she'd be able to talk him off the ledge.
I guess he'd rather listen to a beautiful redhead than a man in tights. Him and me *both*.
INSTITUTE
Thankfully, it doesn't take a *genius* to figure out where he's going.

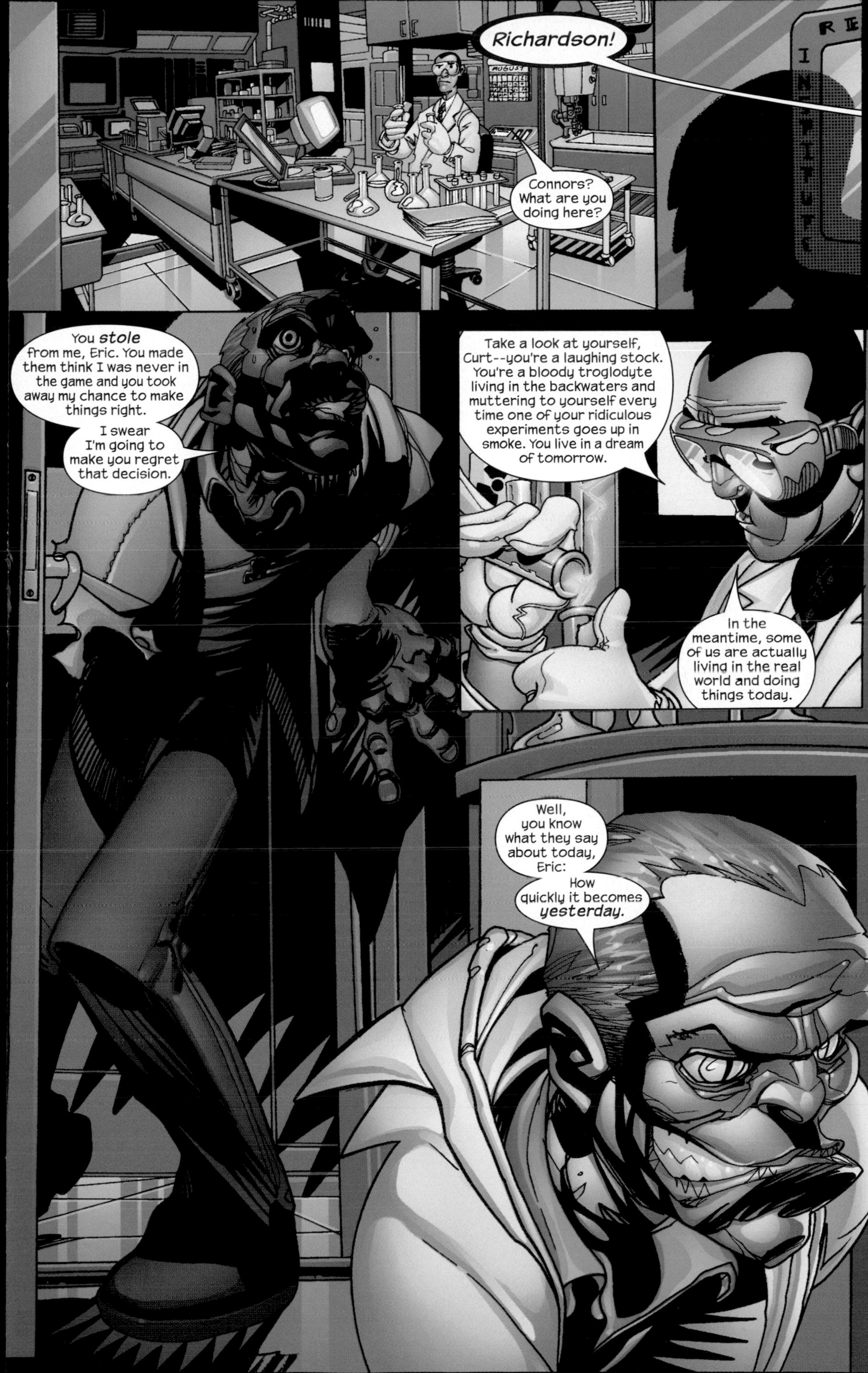
Richardson!
Connors? What are you doing here?
You *stole* from me, Eric. You made them think I was never in the game and you took away my chance to make things right.
I swear I'm going to make you regret that decision.
Take a look at yourself, Curt--you're a laughing stock. You're a bloody troglodyte living in the backwaters and muttering to yourself every time one of your ridiculous experiments goes up in smoke. You live in a dream of tomorrow.
In the meantime, some of us are actually living in the real world and doing things today.
Well, you know what they say about today, Eric:
How quickly it becomes *yesterday*.

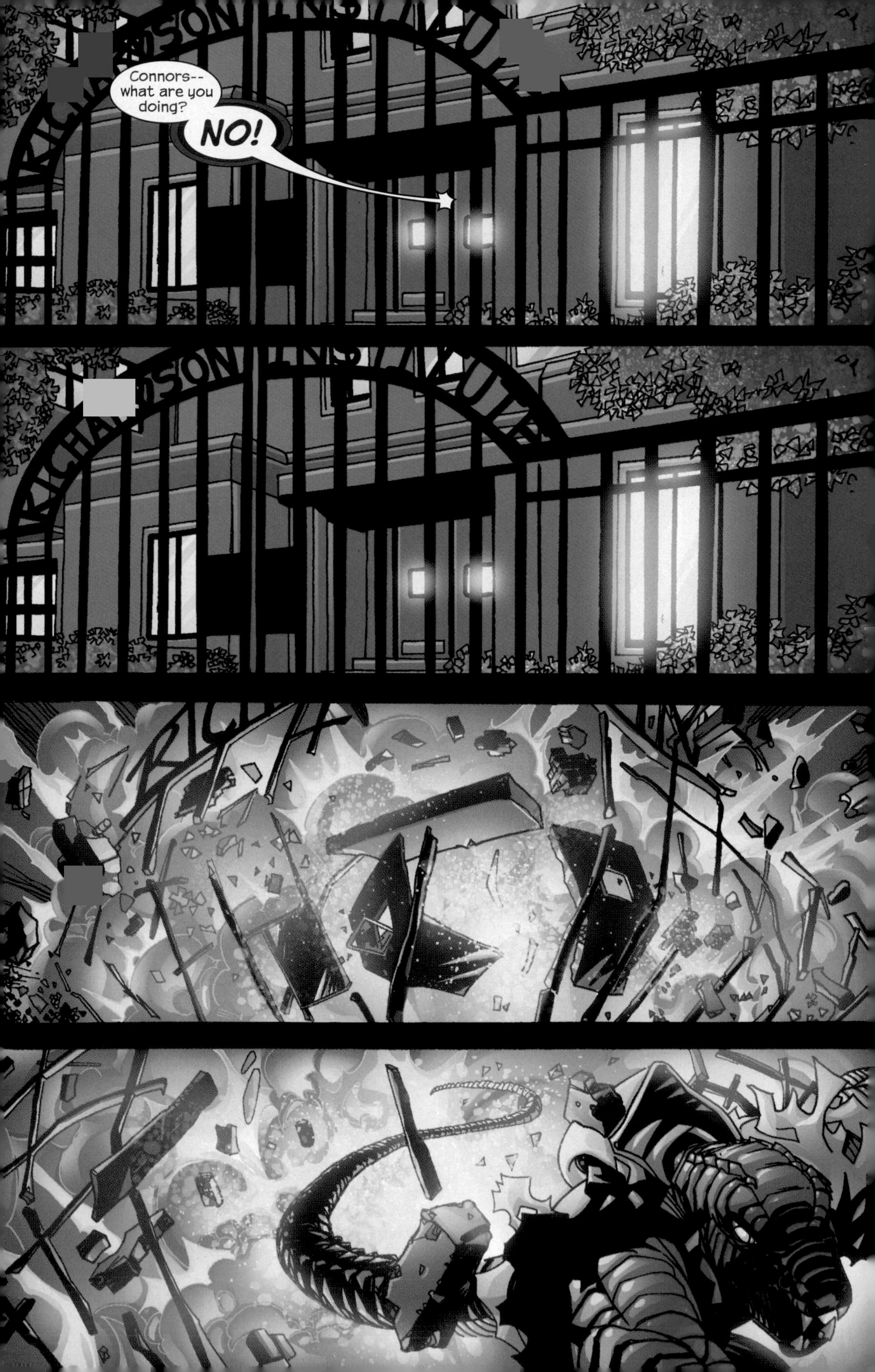
Connors-- what are you doing?
NO!

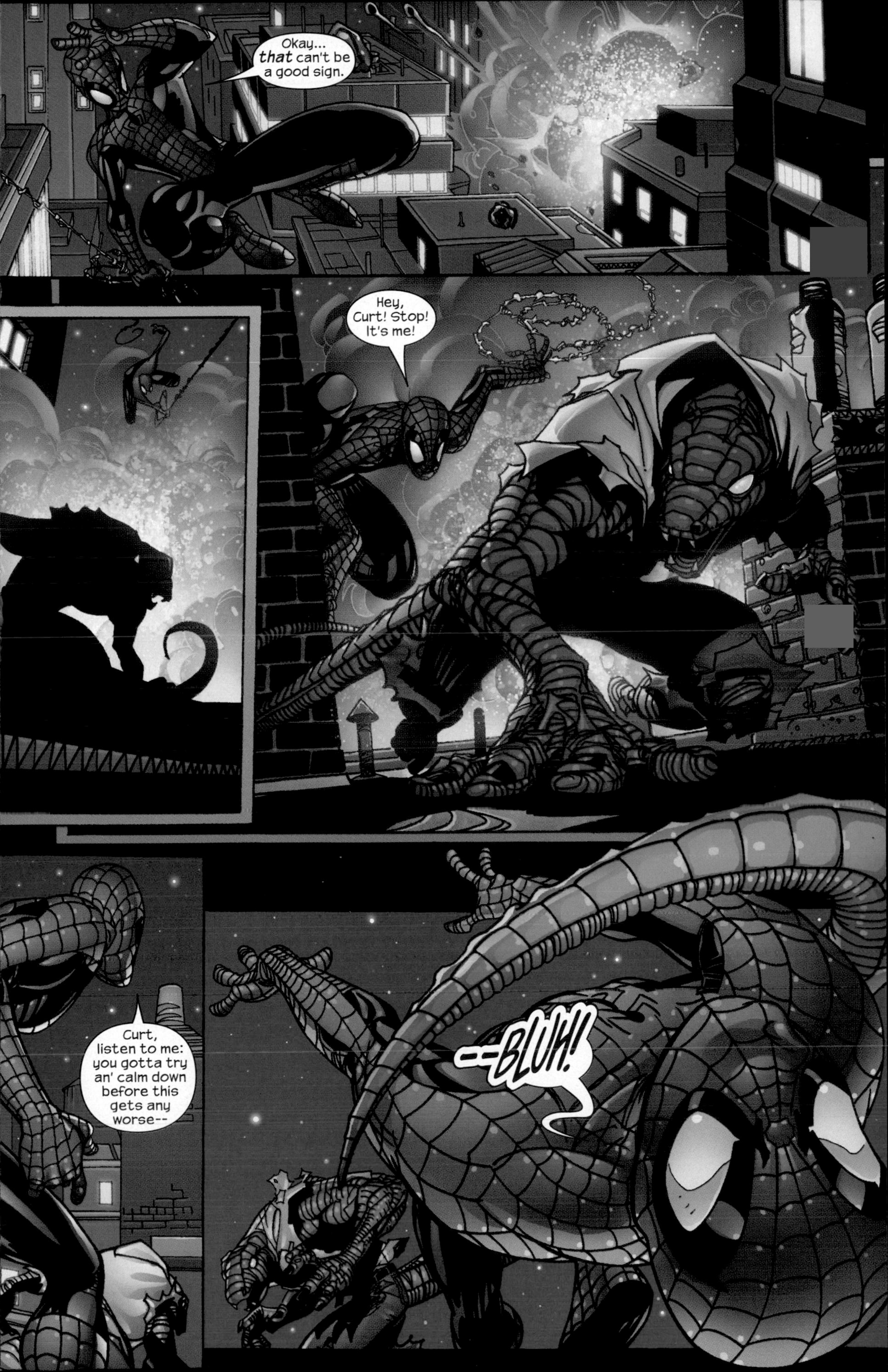

Okay... *that* can't be a good sign.
Hey, Curt! Stop! It's me!
Curt, listen to me: you gotta try an' calm down before this gets any worse--
--BLUH!

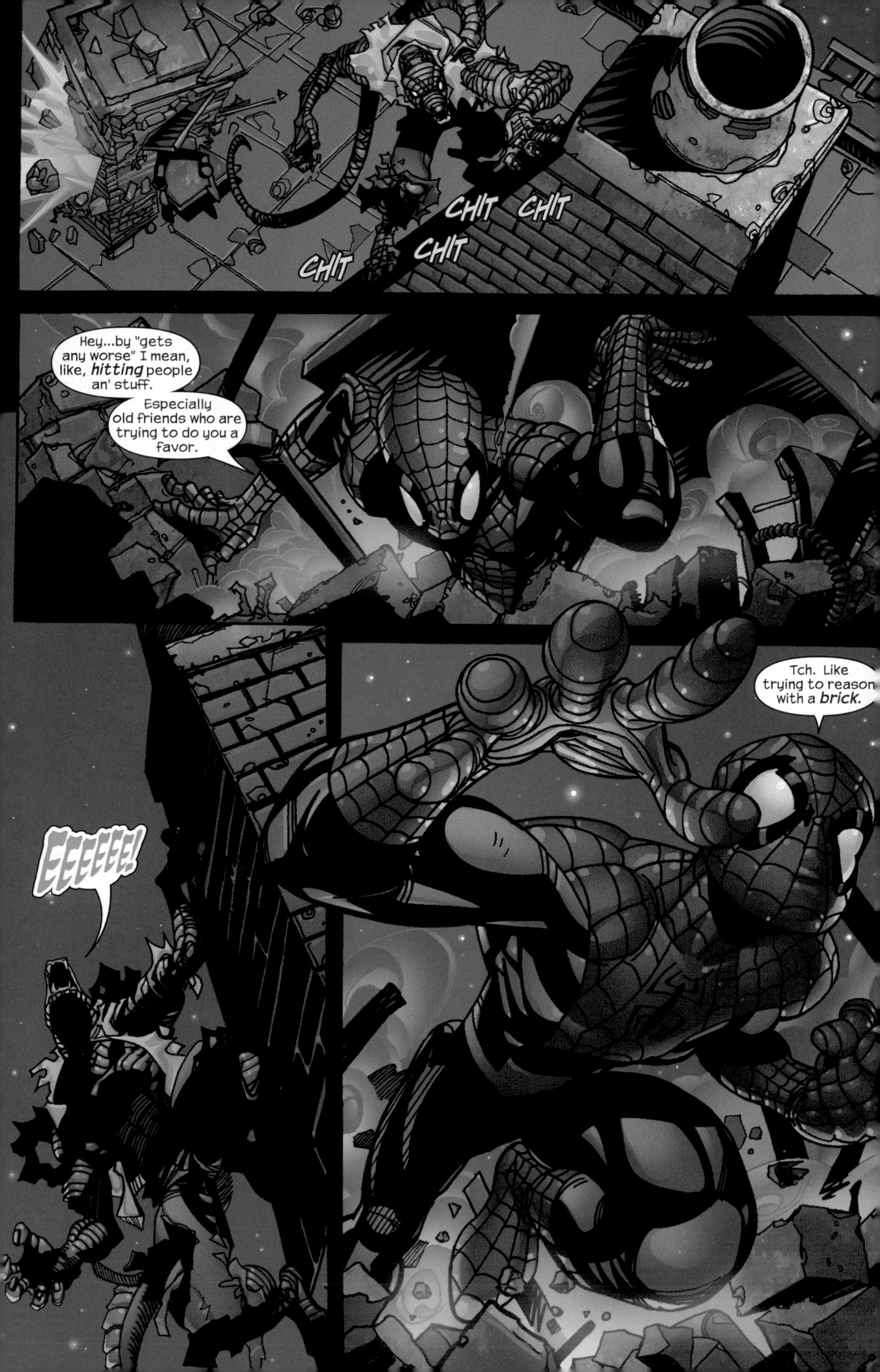
CHIT
CHIT
CHIT
CHIT
Hey...by "gets any worse" I mean, like, *hitting* people an' stuff.
Especially old friends who are trying to do you a favor.
Tch. Like trying to reason with a *brick.*
EEEEEE!

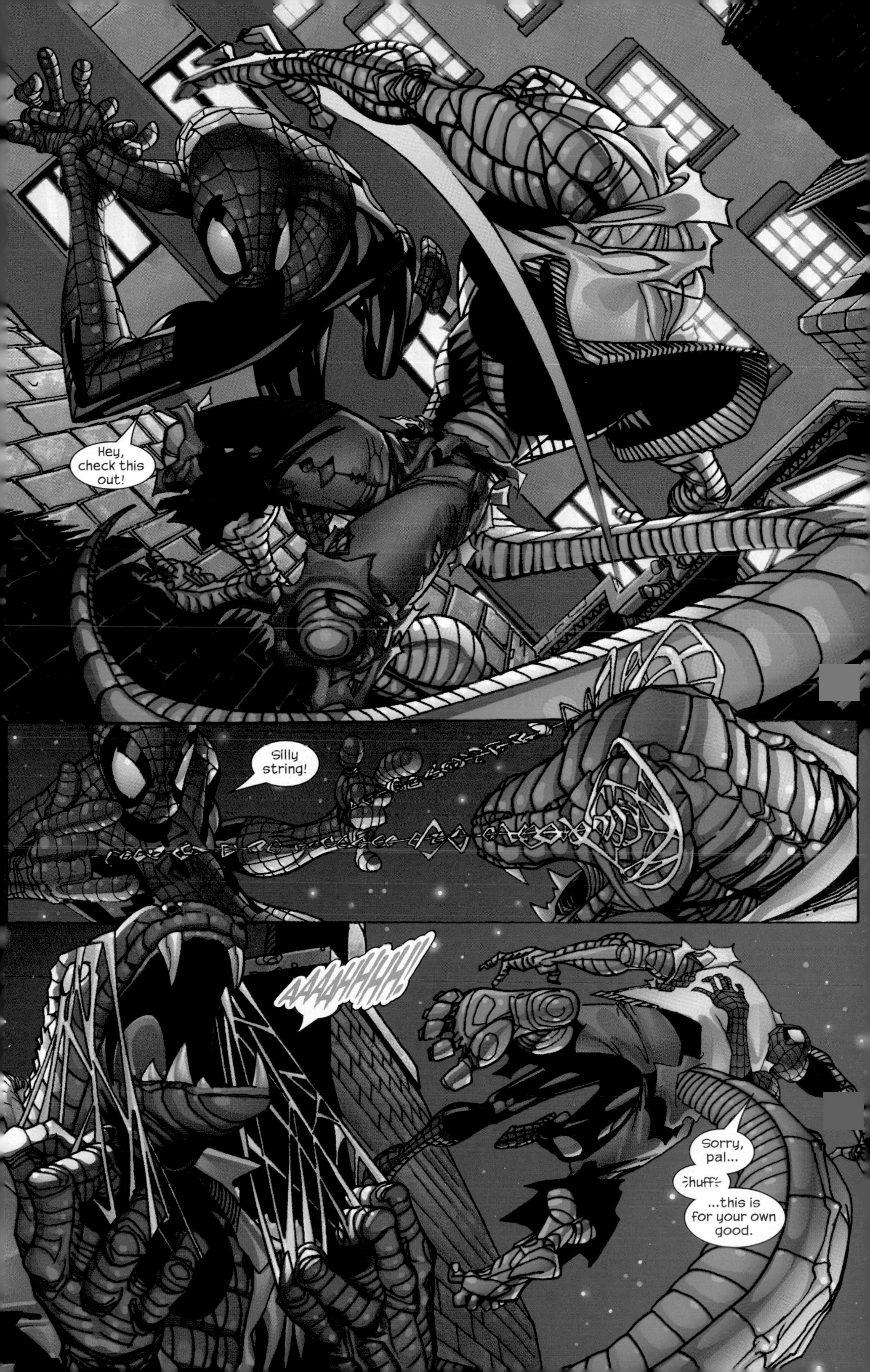
Hey, check this out!
Silly string!
AAAAHHHH!!
Sorry, pal...
huff
...this is for your own good.

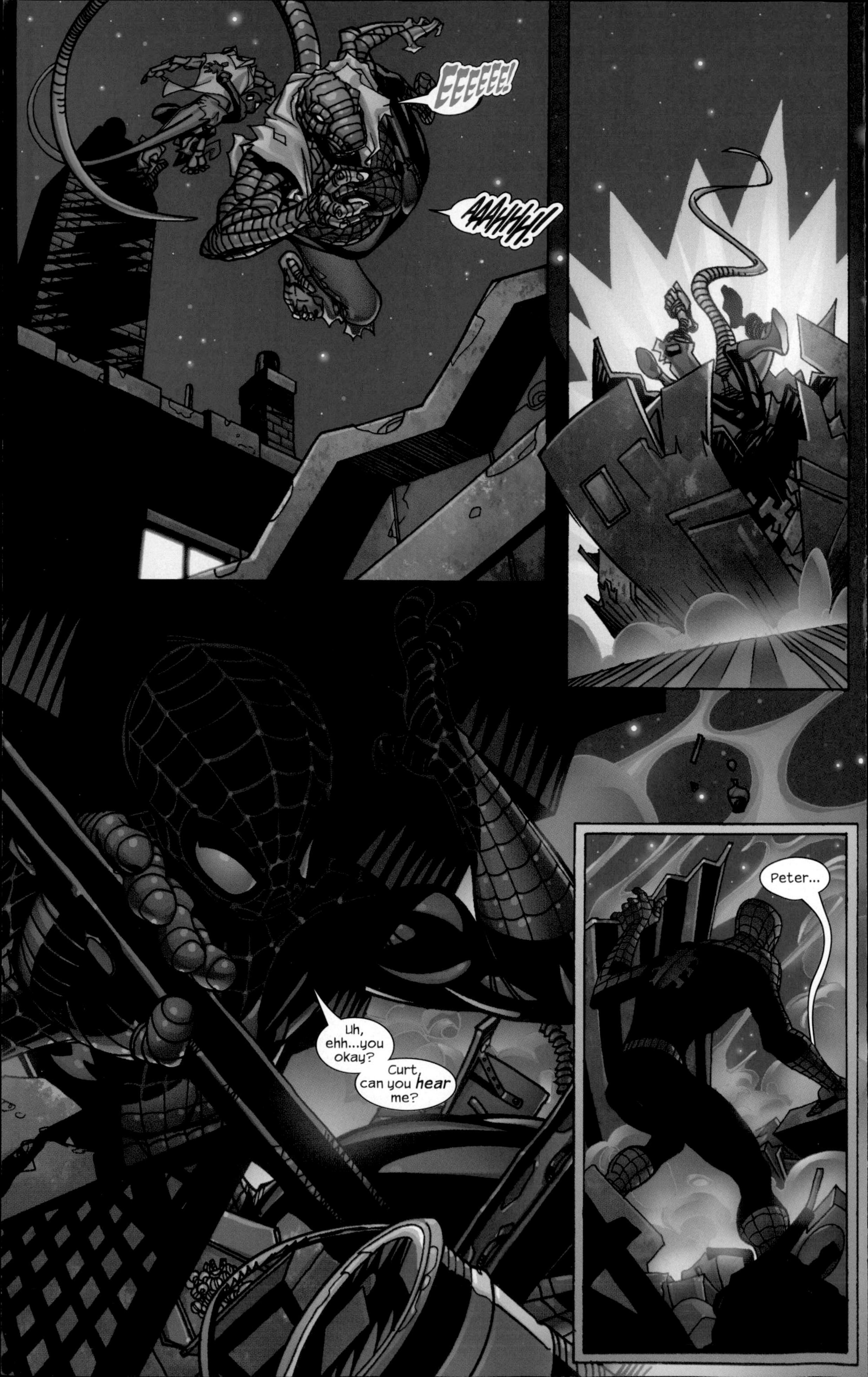
EEEEEE!
AAAHHH!!
Uh, ehh...you okay?
Curt, can you *hear* me?
Peter...

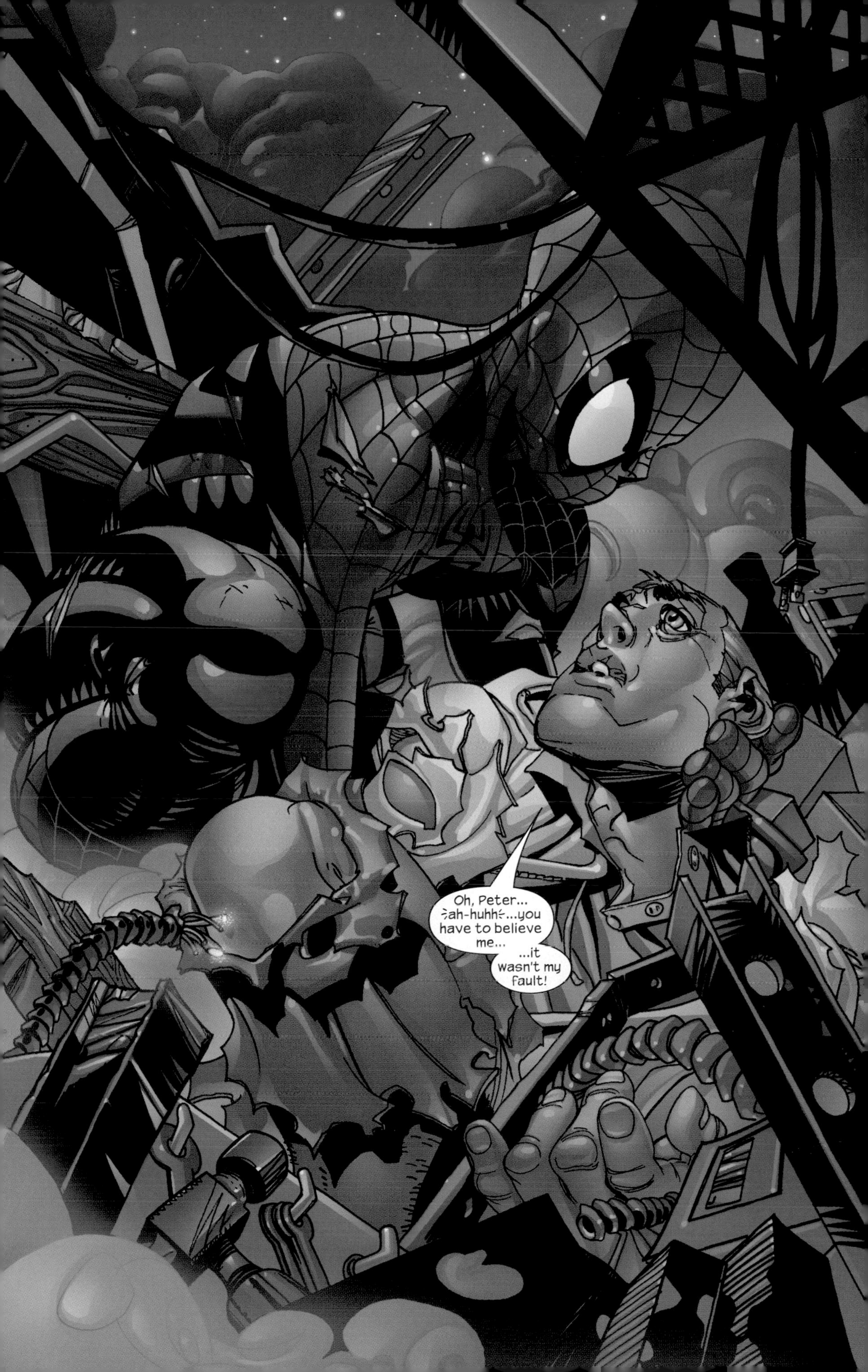
Oh, Peter... -ah-huhh- ...you have to believe me...
...it wasn't my fault!

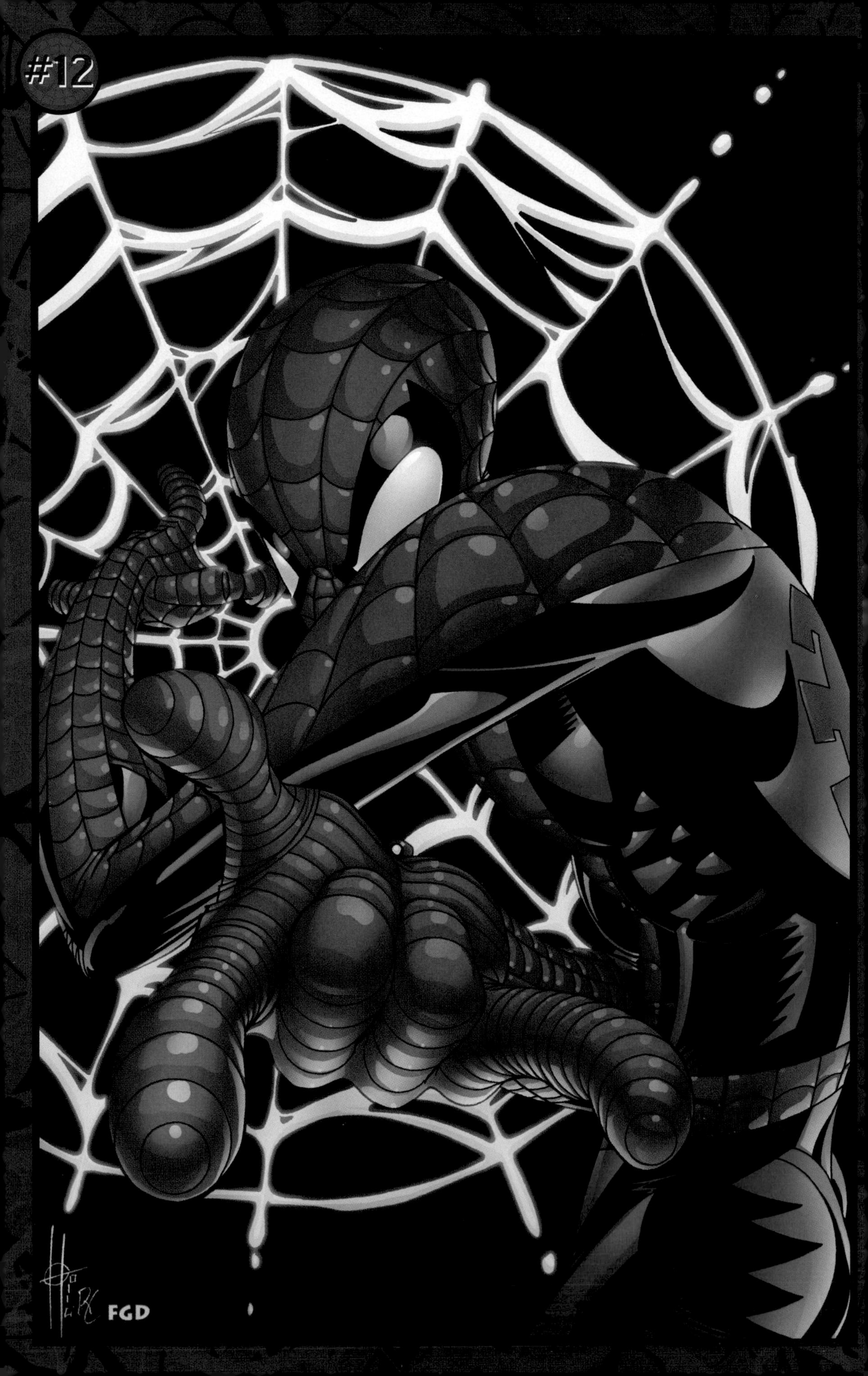
#12
FGD

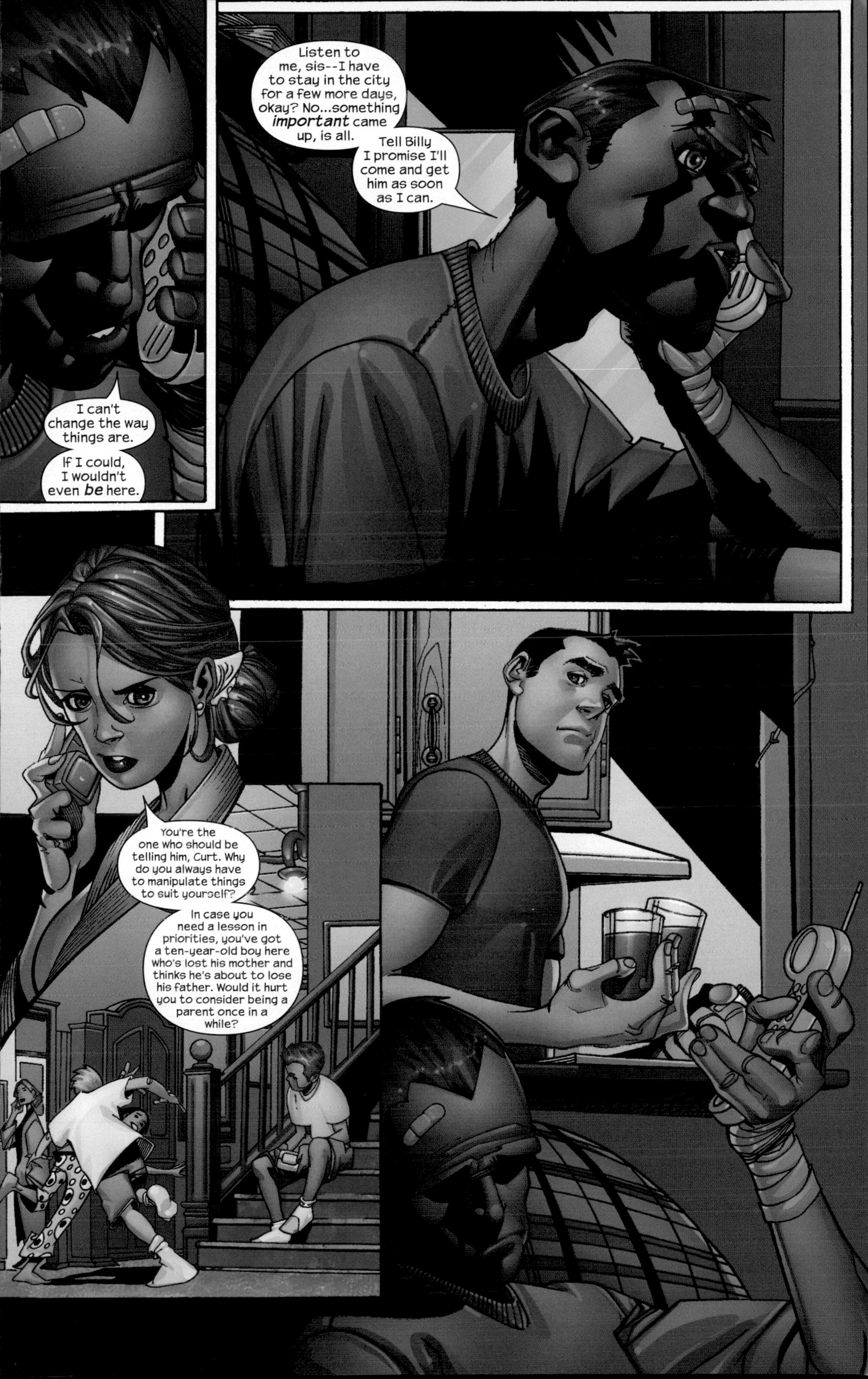
Listen to me, sis--I have to stay in the city for a few more days, okay? No...something *important* came up, is all.
Tell Billy I promise I'll come and get him as soon as I can.
I can't change the way things are.
If I could, I wouldn't even *be* here.
You're the one who should be telling him, Curt. Why do you always have to manipulate things to suit yourself?
In case you need a lesson in priorities, you've got a ten-year-old boy here who's lost his mother and thinks he's about to lose his father. Would it hurt you to consider being a parent once in a while?

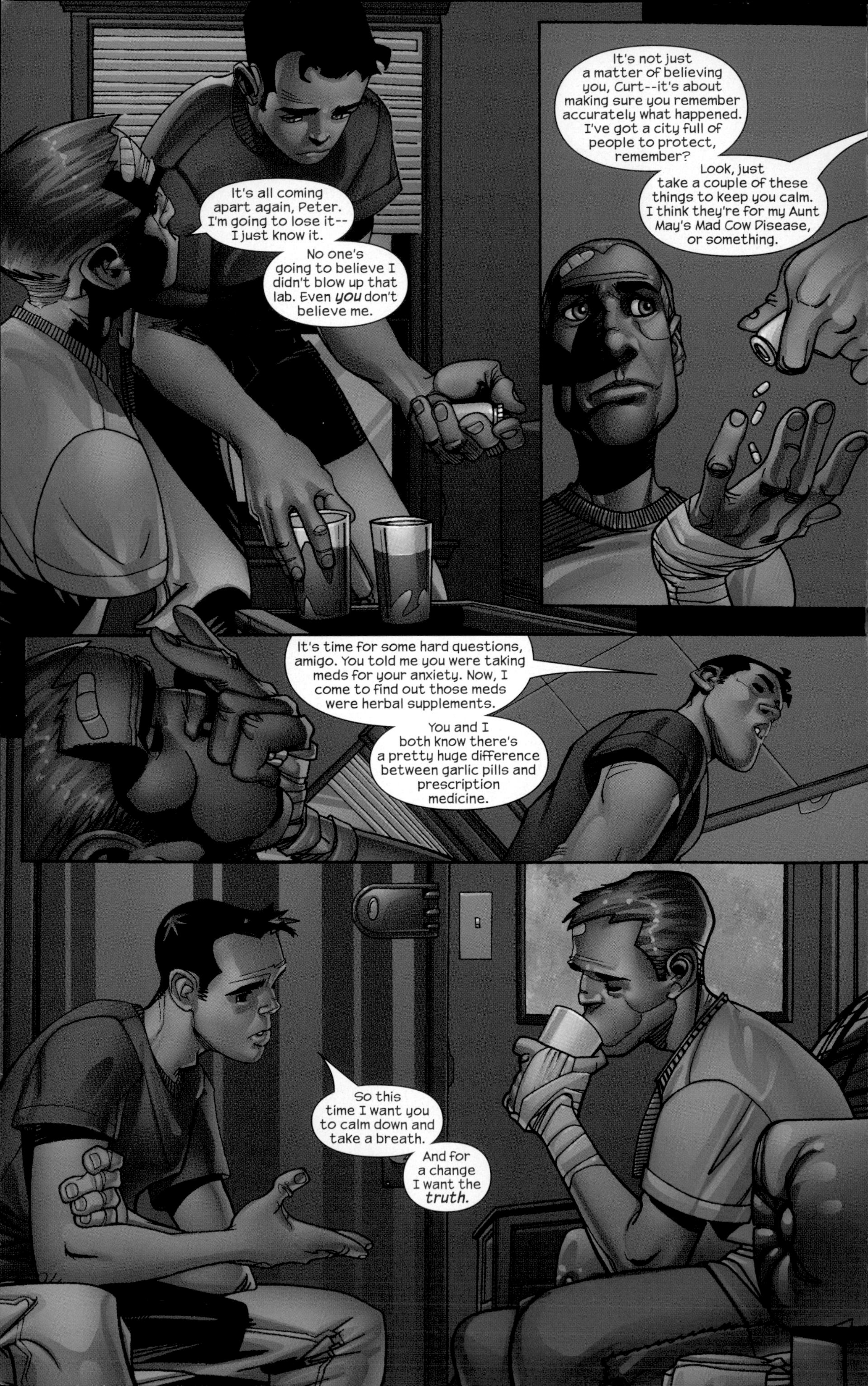
It's all coming apart again, Peter. I'm going to lose it--I just know it.
No one's going to believe I didn't blow up that lab. Even *you* don't believe me.
It's not just a matter of believing you, Curt--it's about making sure you remember accurately what happened. I've got a city full of people to protect, remember?
Look, just take a couple of these things to keep you calm. I think they're for my Aunt May's Mad Cow Disease, or something.
It's time for some hard questions, amigo. You told me you were taking meds for your anxiety. Now, I come to find out those meds were herbal supplements.
You and I both know there's a pretty huge difference between garlic pills and prescription medicine.
So this time I want you to calm down and take a breath.
And for a change I want the *truth.*

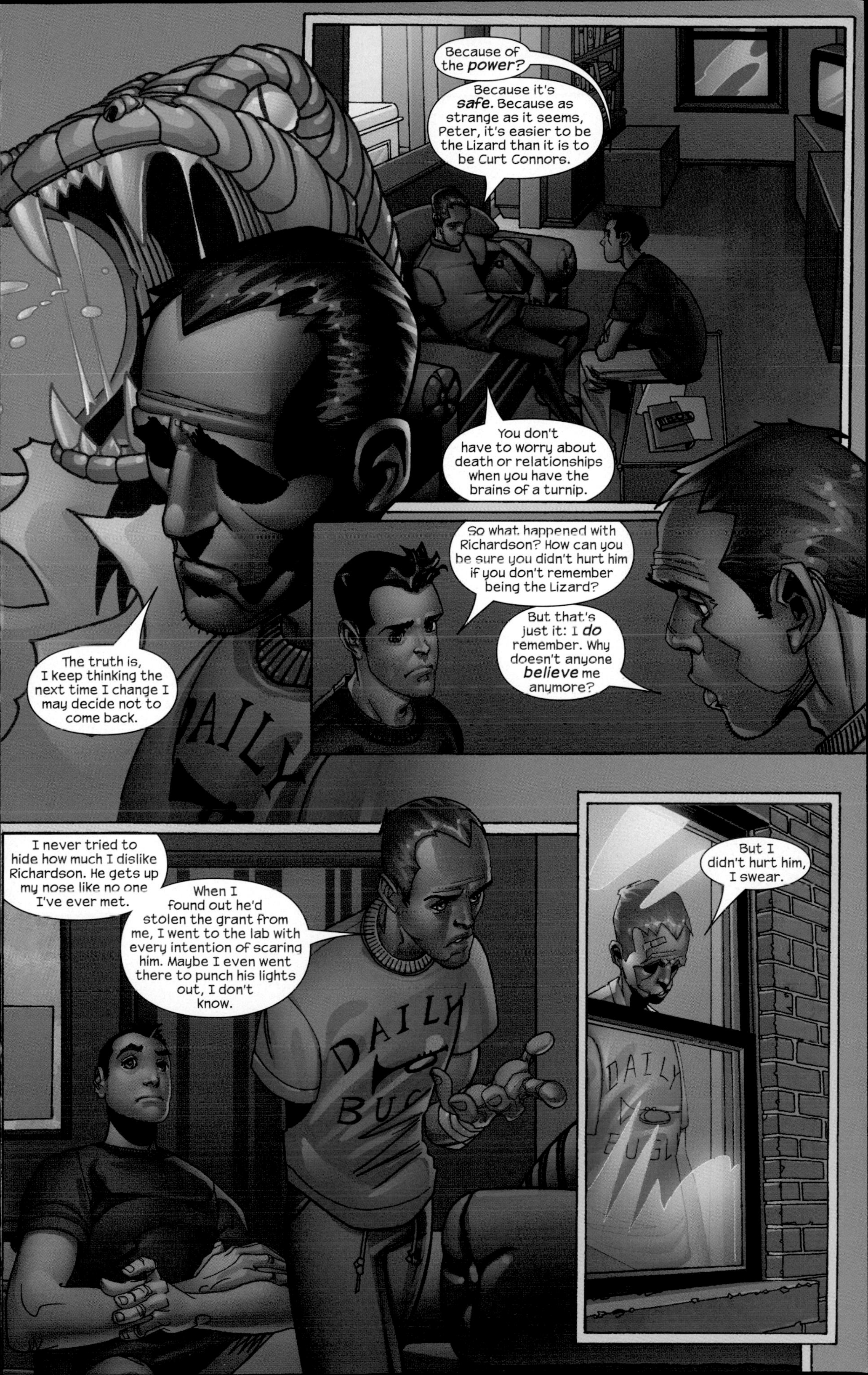
Because of the *power?*
Because it's *safe.* Because as strange as it seems, Peter, it's easier to be the Lizard than it is to be Curt Connors.
You don't have to worry about death or relationships when you have the brains of a turnip.
The truth is, I keep thinking the next time I change I may decide not to come back.
So what happened with Richardson? How can you be sure you didn't hurt him if you don't remember being the Lizard?
But that's just it: I *do* remember. Why doesn't anyone *believe* me anymore?
I never tried to hide how much I dislike Richardson. He gets up my nose like no one I've ever met.
When I found out he'd stolen the grant from me, I went to the lab with every intention of scaring him. Maybe I even went there to punch his lights out, I don't know.
But I didn't hurt him, I swear.

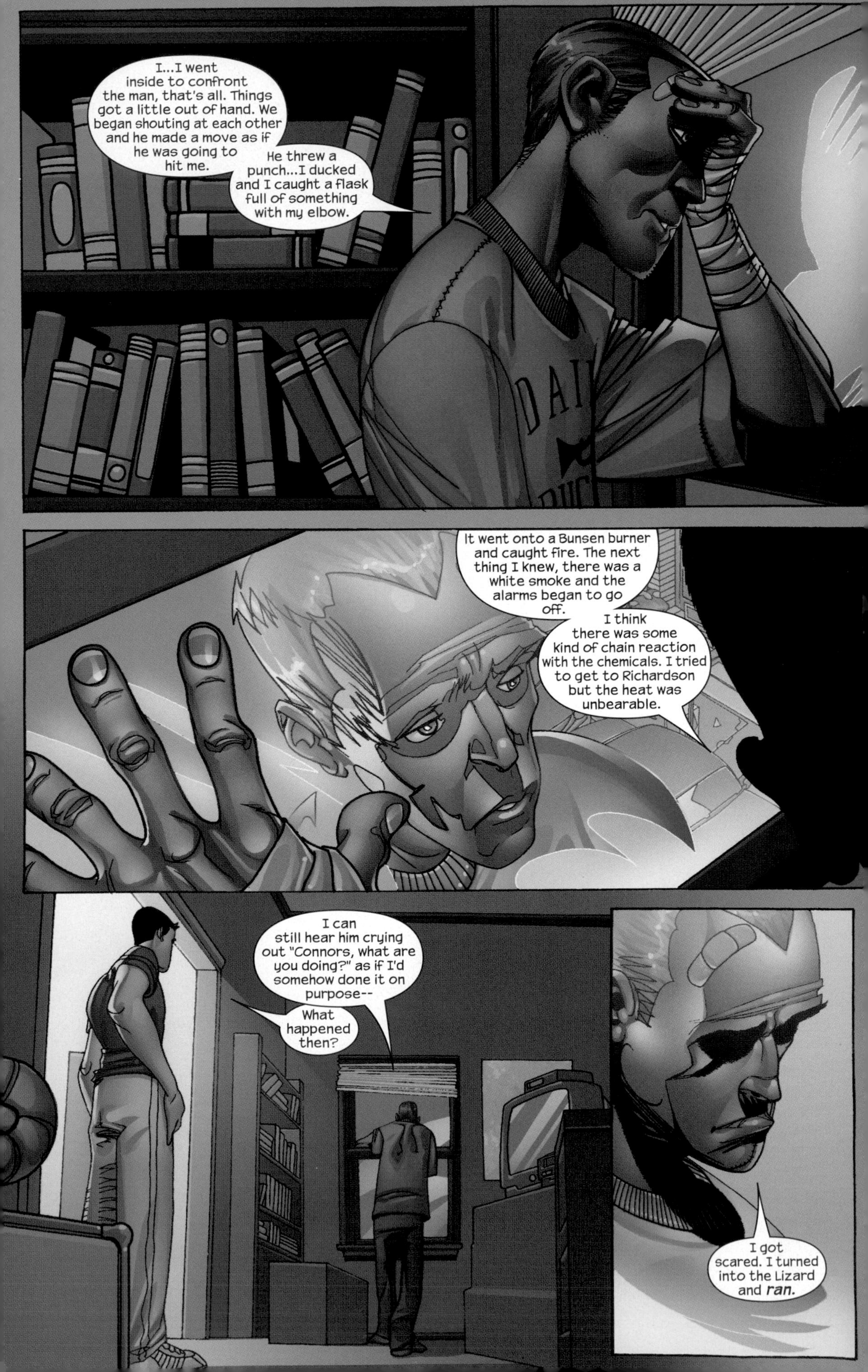
I...I went inside to confront the man, that's all. Things got a little out of hand. We began shouting at each other and he made a move as if he was going to hit me.
He threw a punch...I ducked and I caught a flask full of something with my elbow.
It went onto a Bunsen burner and caught fire. The next thing I knew, there was a white smoke and the alarms began to go off.
I think there was some kind of chain reaction with the chemicals. I tried to get to Richardson but the heat was unbearable.
I can still hear him crying out "Connors, what are you doing?" as if I'd somehow done it on purpose--
What happened then?
I got scared. I turned into the Lizard and *ran.*

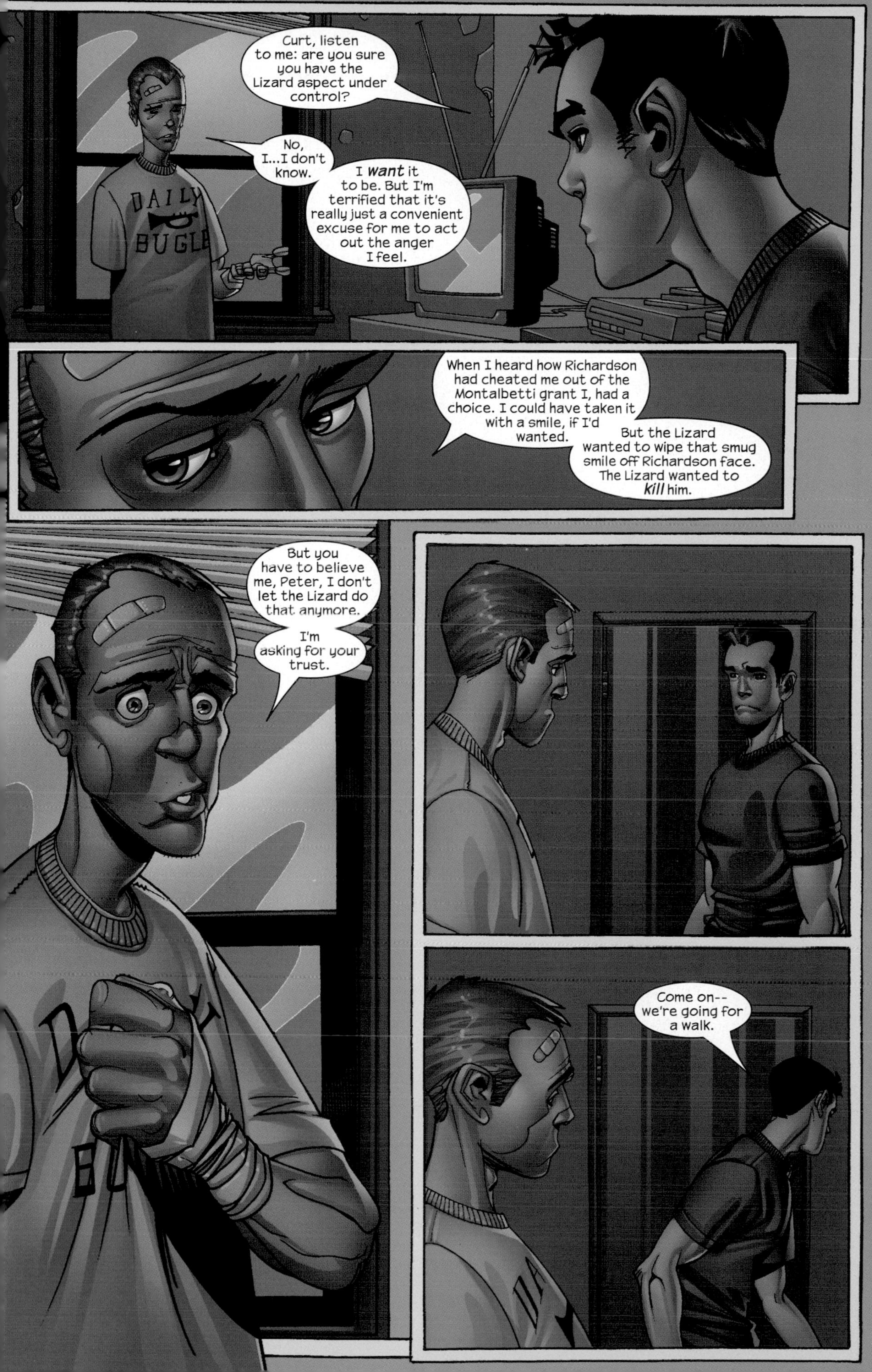
Curt, listen to me: are you sure you have the Lizard aspect under control?
No, I...I don't know.
I *want* it to be. But I'm terrified that it's really just a convenient excuse for me to act out the anger I feel.
When I heard how Richardson had cheated me out of the Montalbetti grant I, had a choice. I could have taken it with a smile, if I'd wanted.
But the Lizard wanted to wipe that smug smile off Richardson face. The Lizard wanted to *kill* him.
But you have to believe me, Peter, I don't let the Lizard do that anymore.
I'm asking for your trust.
Come on-- we're going for a walk.

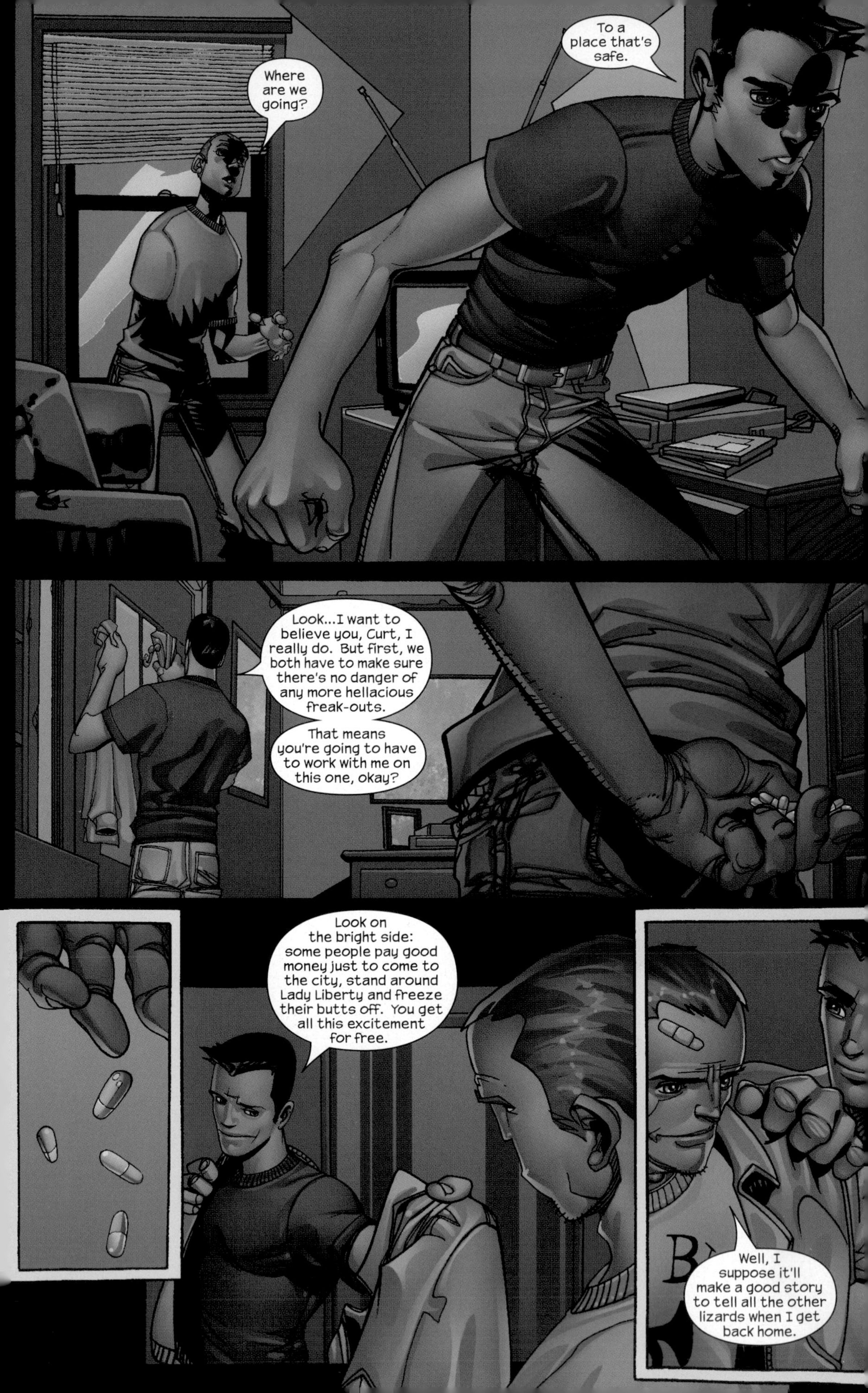
Where are we going?
To a place that's safe.
Look...I want to believe you, Curt, I really do. But first, we both have to make sure there's no danger of any more hellacious freak-outs.
That means you're going to have to work with me on this one, okay?
Look on the bright side: some people pay good money just to come to the city, stand around Lady Liberty and freeze their butts off. You get all this excitement for free.
Well, I suppose it'll make a good story to tell all the other lizards when I get back home.

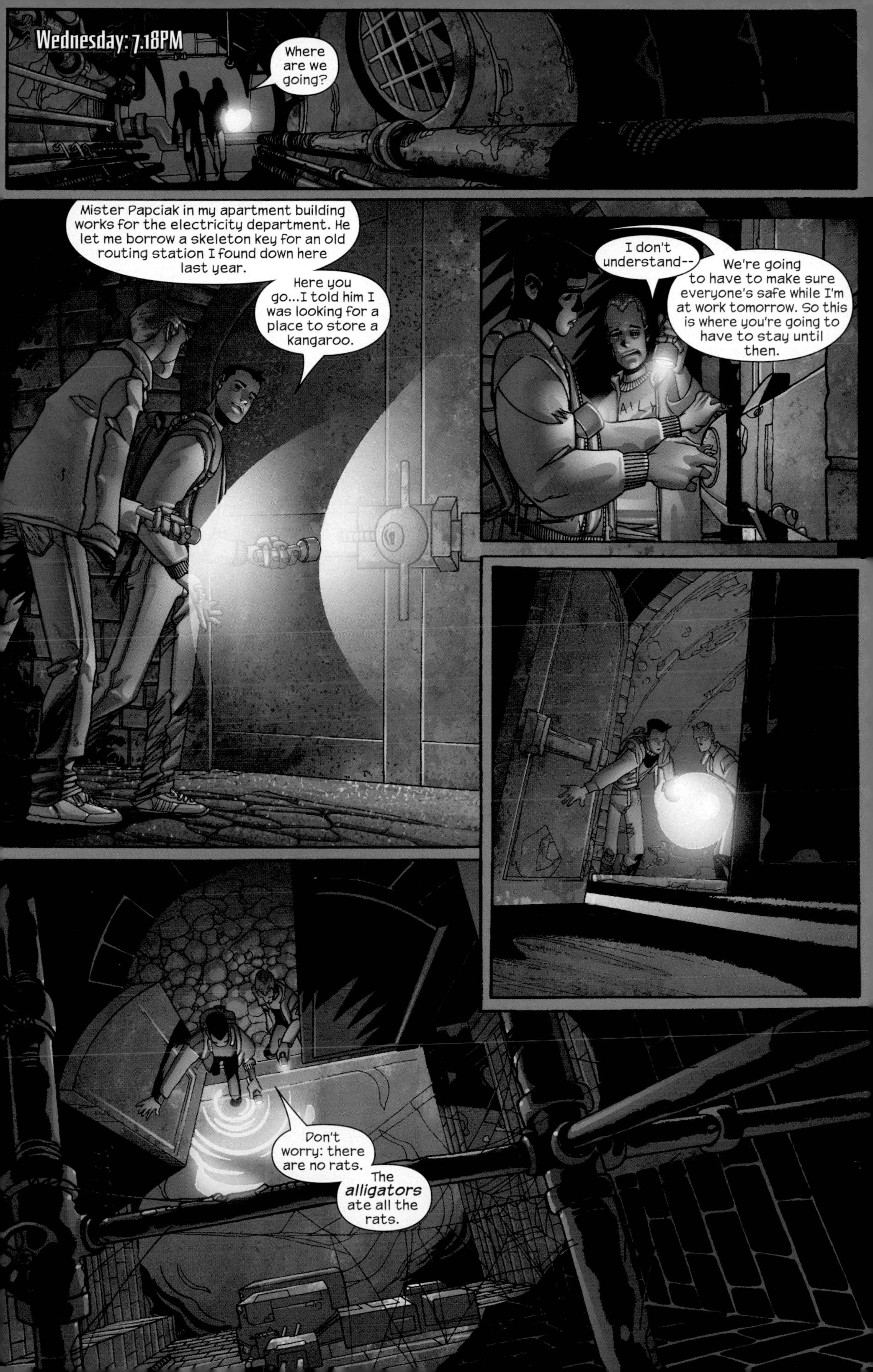
Wednesday: 7.18PM
Where are we going?
Mister Papciak in my apartment building works for the electricity department. He let me borrow a skeleton key for an old routing station I found down here last year.
Here you go...I told him I was looking for a place to store a kangaroo.
I don't understand--
We're going to have to make sure everyone's safe while I'm at work tomorrow. So this is where you're going to have to stay until then.
Don't worry: there are no rats.
The *alligators* ate all the rats.

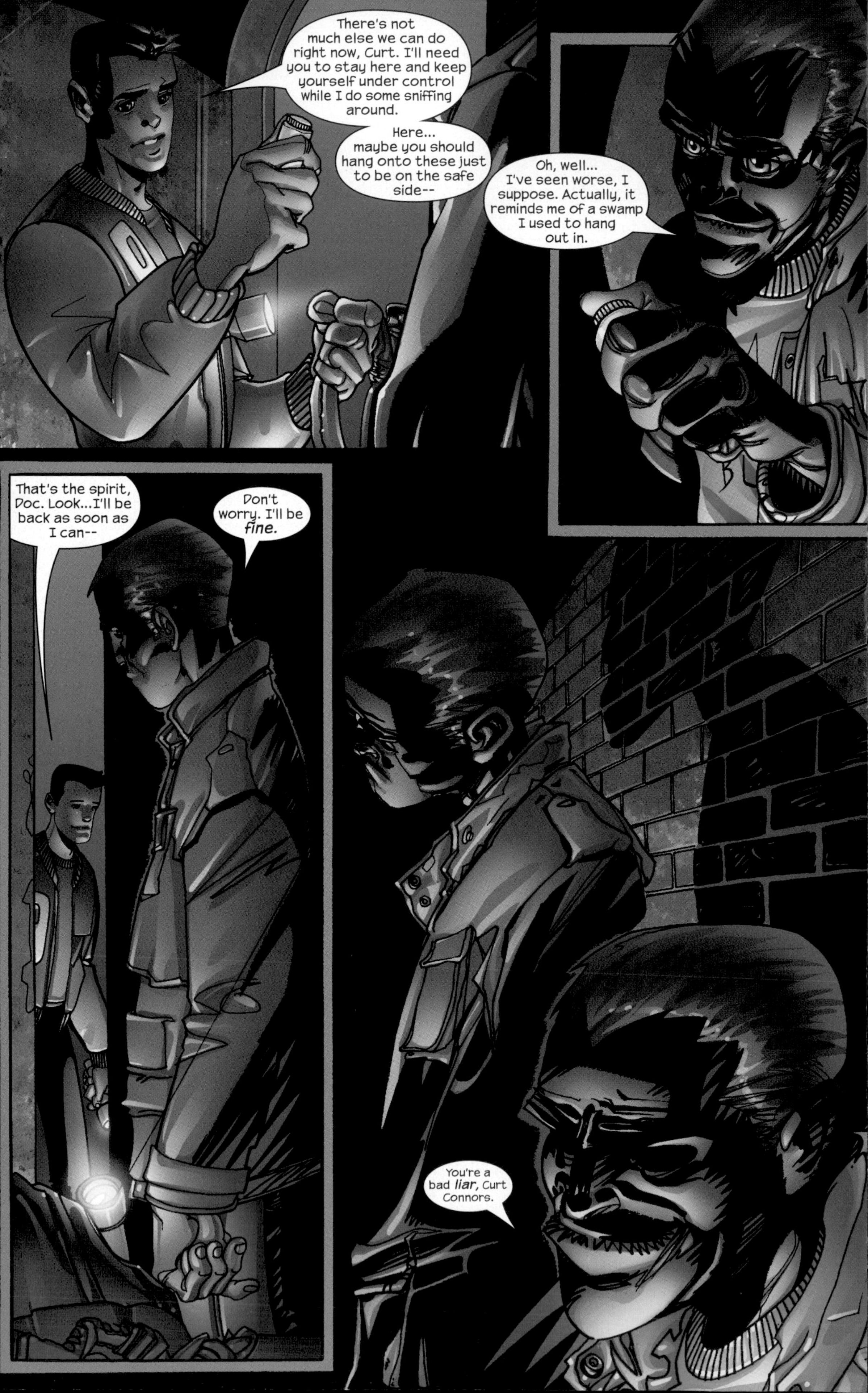
There's not much else we can do right now, Curt. I'll need you to stay here and keep yourself under control while I do some sniffing around.
Here... maybe you should hang onto these just to be on the safe side--
Oh, well... I've seen worse, I suppose. Actually, it reminds me of a swamp I used to hang out in.
That's the spirit, Doc. Look...I'll be back as soon as I can--
Don't worry. I'll be *fine.*
You're a bad *liar,* Curt Connors.

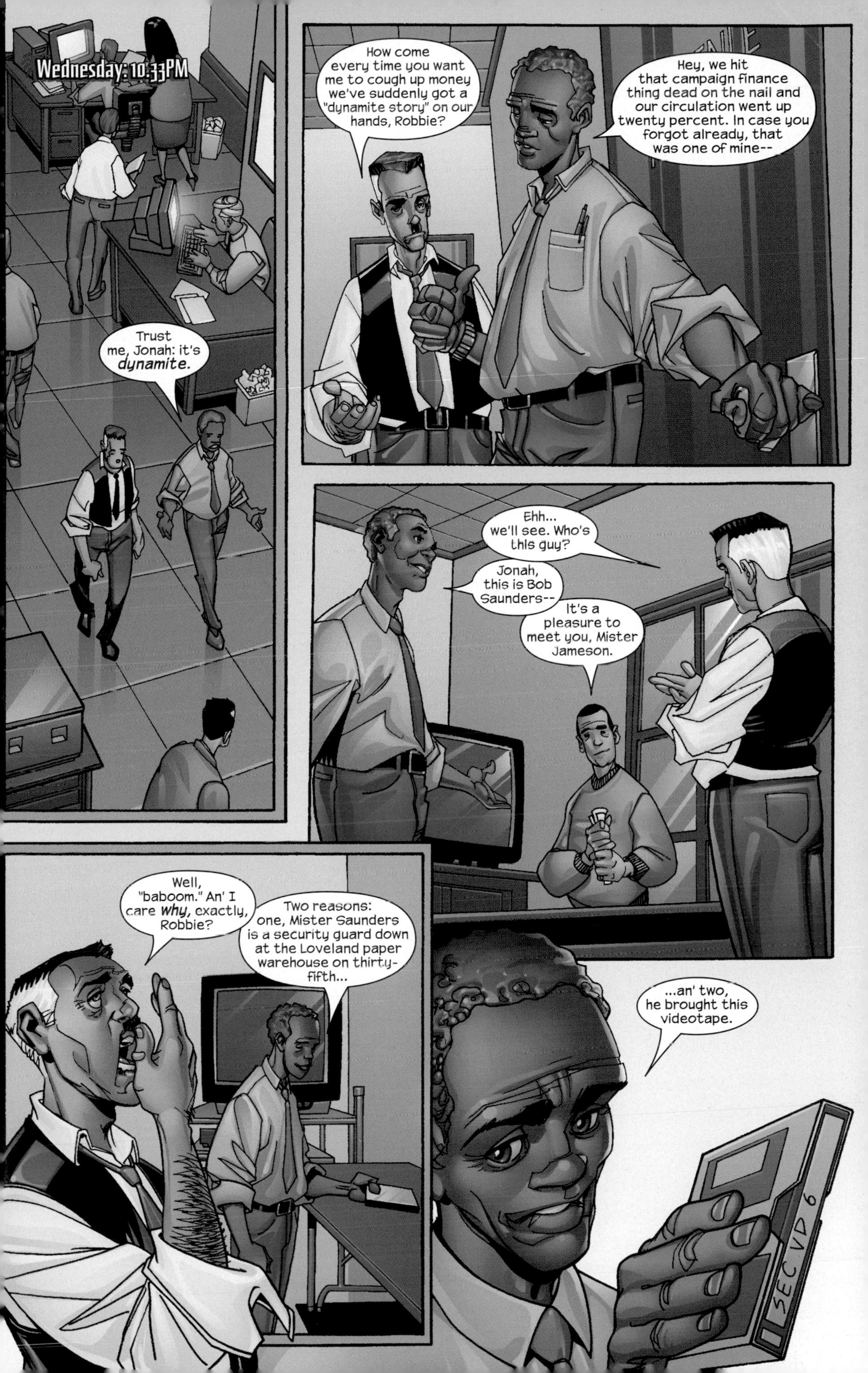
Wednesday: 10:33PM
Trust me, Jonah: it's *dynamite.*
How come every time you want me to cough up money we've suddenly got a "dynamite story" on our hands, Robbie?
Hey, we hit that campaign finance thing dead on the nail and our circulation went up twenty percent. In case you forgot already, that was one of mine--
Ehh... we'll see. Who's this guy?
Jonah, this is Bob Saunders--
It's a pleasure to meet you, Mister Jameson.
Well, "baboom." An' I care *why,* exactly, Robbie?
Two reasons: one, Mister Saunders is a security guard down at the Loveland paper warehouse on thirty-fifth...
...an' two, he brought this videotape.
SEC VD 6

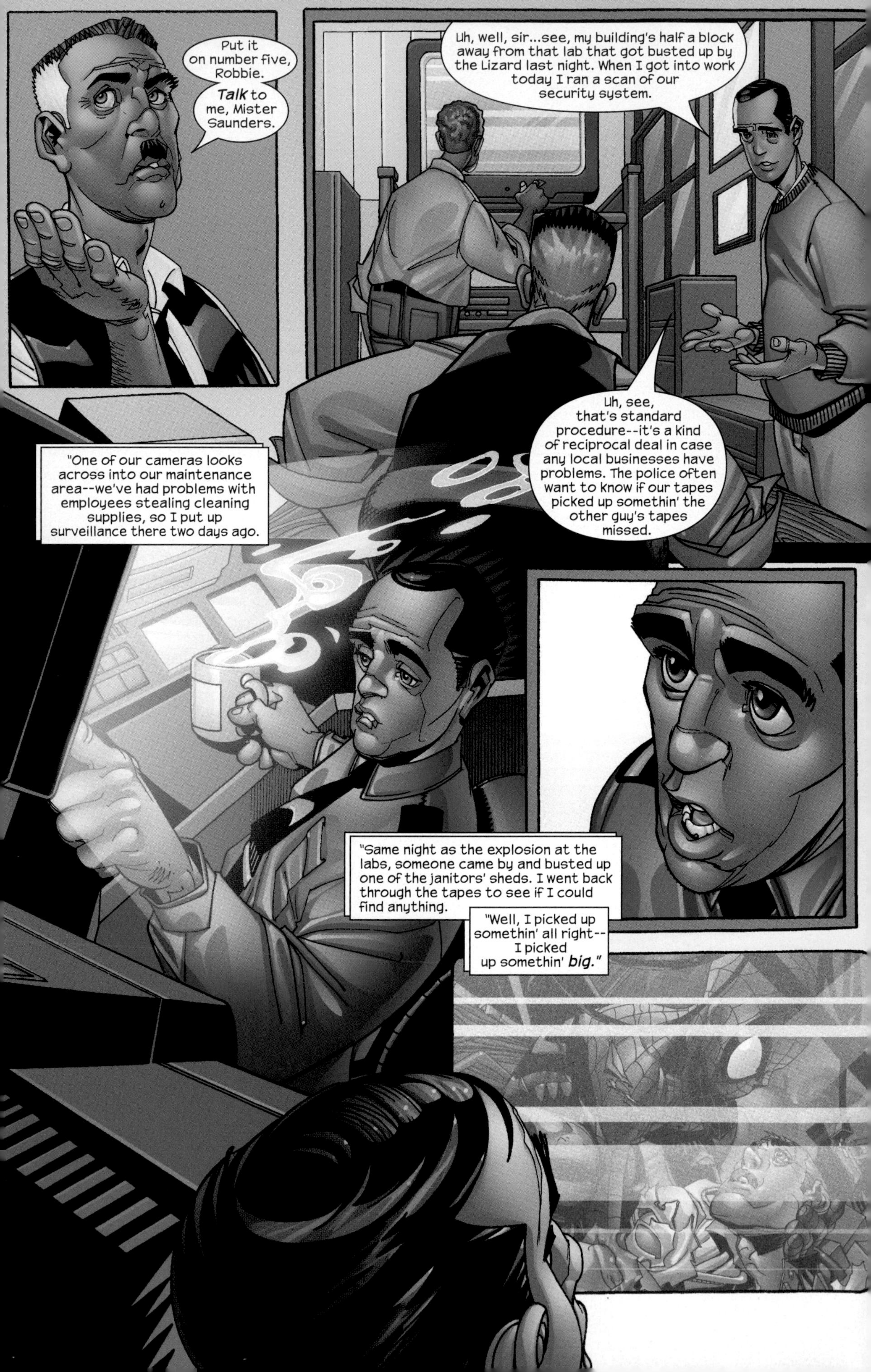
Put it on number five, Robbie.
Talk to me, Mister Saunders.
Uh, well, sir...see, my building's half a block away from that lab that got busted up by the Lizard last night. When I got into work today I ran a scan of our security system.
"One of our cameras looks across into our maintenance area--we've had problems with employees stealing cleaning supplies, so I put up surveillance there two days ago.
Uh, see, that's standard procedure--it's a kind of reciprocal deal in case any local businesses have problems. The police often want to know if our tapes picked up somethin' the other guy's tapes missed.
"Same night as the explosion at the labs, someone came by and busted up one of the janitors' sheds. I went back through the tapes to see if I could find anything.
"Well, I picked up somethin' all right-- I picked up somethin' *big.*"

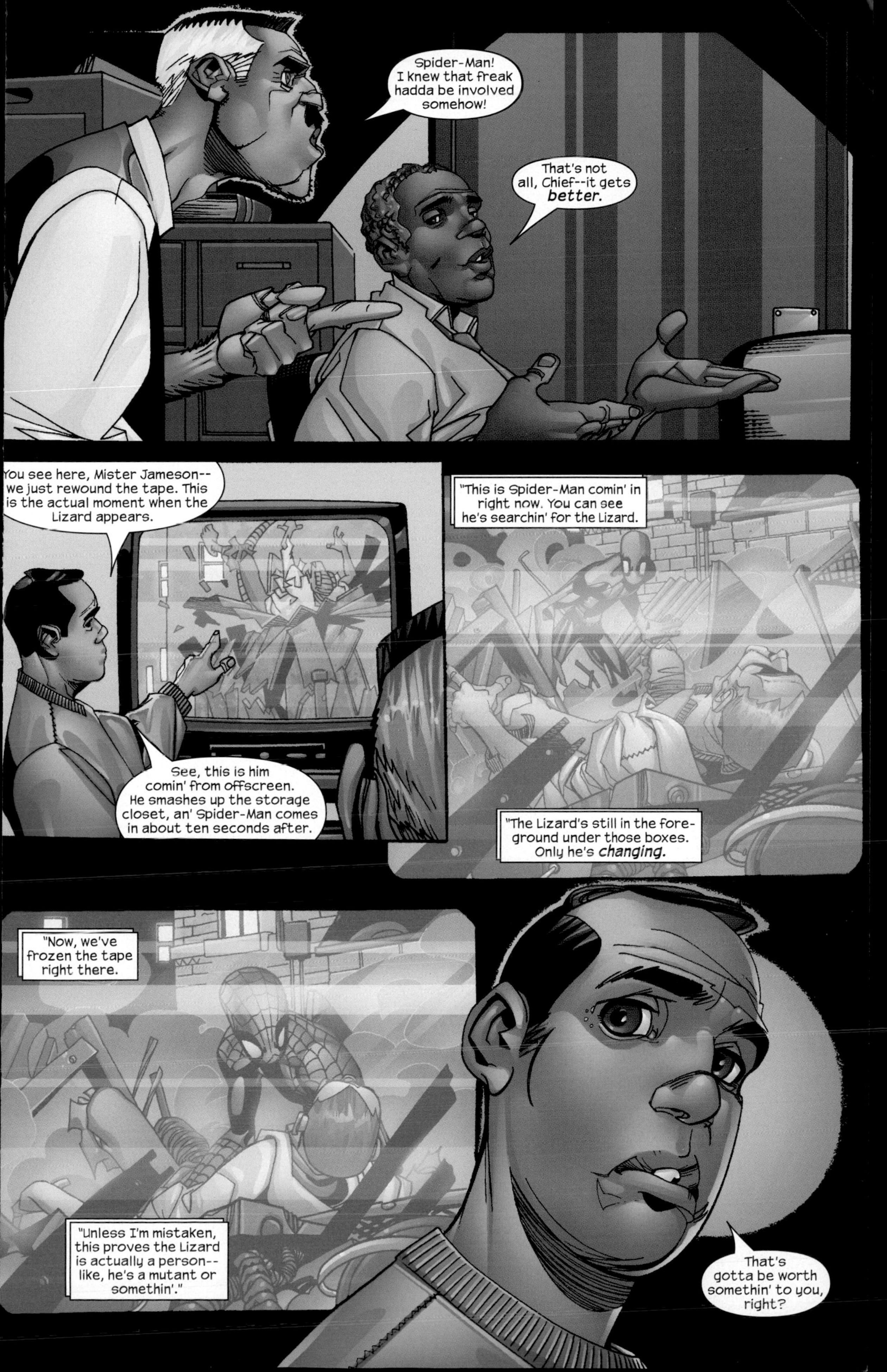

Spider-Man! I knew that freak hadda be involved somehow!
That's not all, Chief--it gets *better*.
You see here, Mister Jameson-- we just rewound the tape. This is the actual moment when the Lizard appears.
See, this is him comin' from offscreen. He smashes up the storage closet, an' Spider-Man comes in about ten seconds after.
"This is Spider-Man comin' in right now. You can see he's searchin' for the Lizard.
"The Lizard's still in the fore-ground under those boxes. Only he's *changing.*
"Now, we've frozen the tape right there.
"Unless I'm mistaken, this proves the Lizard is actually a person-- like, he's a mutant or somethin'."
That's gotta be worth somethin' to you, right?

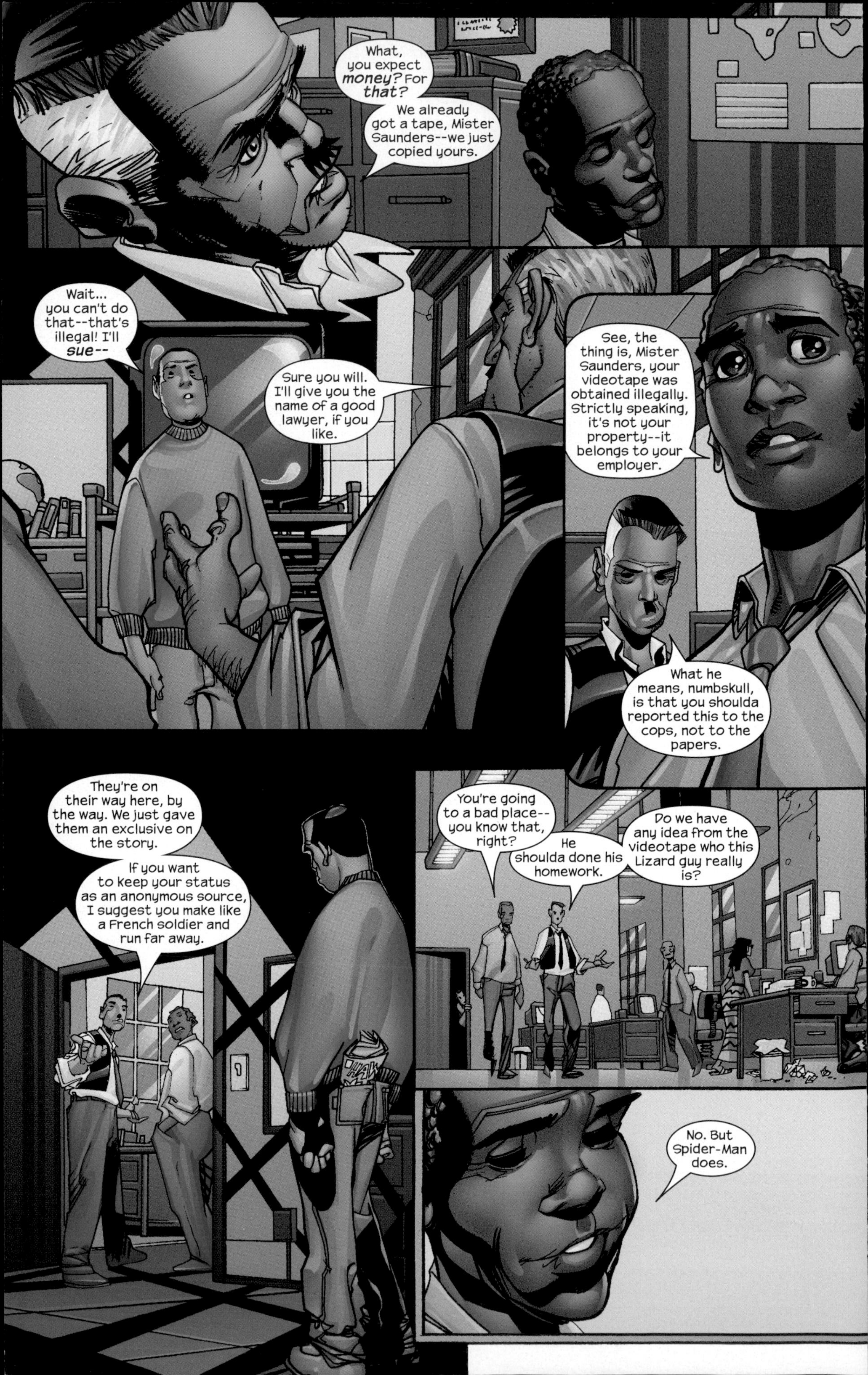
What, you expect money? For that?
We already got a tape, Mister Saunders--we just copied yours.
Wait... you can't do that--that's illegal! I'll sue--
Sure you will. I'll give you the name of a good lawyer, if you like.
See, the thing is, Mister Saunders, your videotape was obtained illegally. Strictly speaking, it's not your property--it belongs to your employer.
What he means, numbskull, is that you shoulda reported this to the cops, not to the papers.
They're on their way here, by the way. We just gave them an exclusive on the story.
If you want to keep your status as an anonymous source, I suggest you make like a French soldier and run far away.
You're going to a bad place--you know that, right?
He shoulda done his homework.
Do we have any idea from the videotape who this Lizard guy really is?
No. But Spider-Man does.

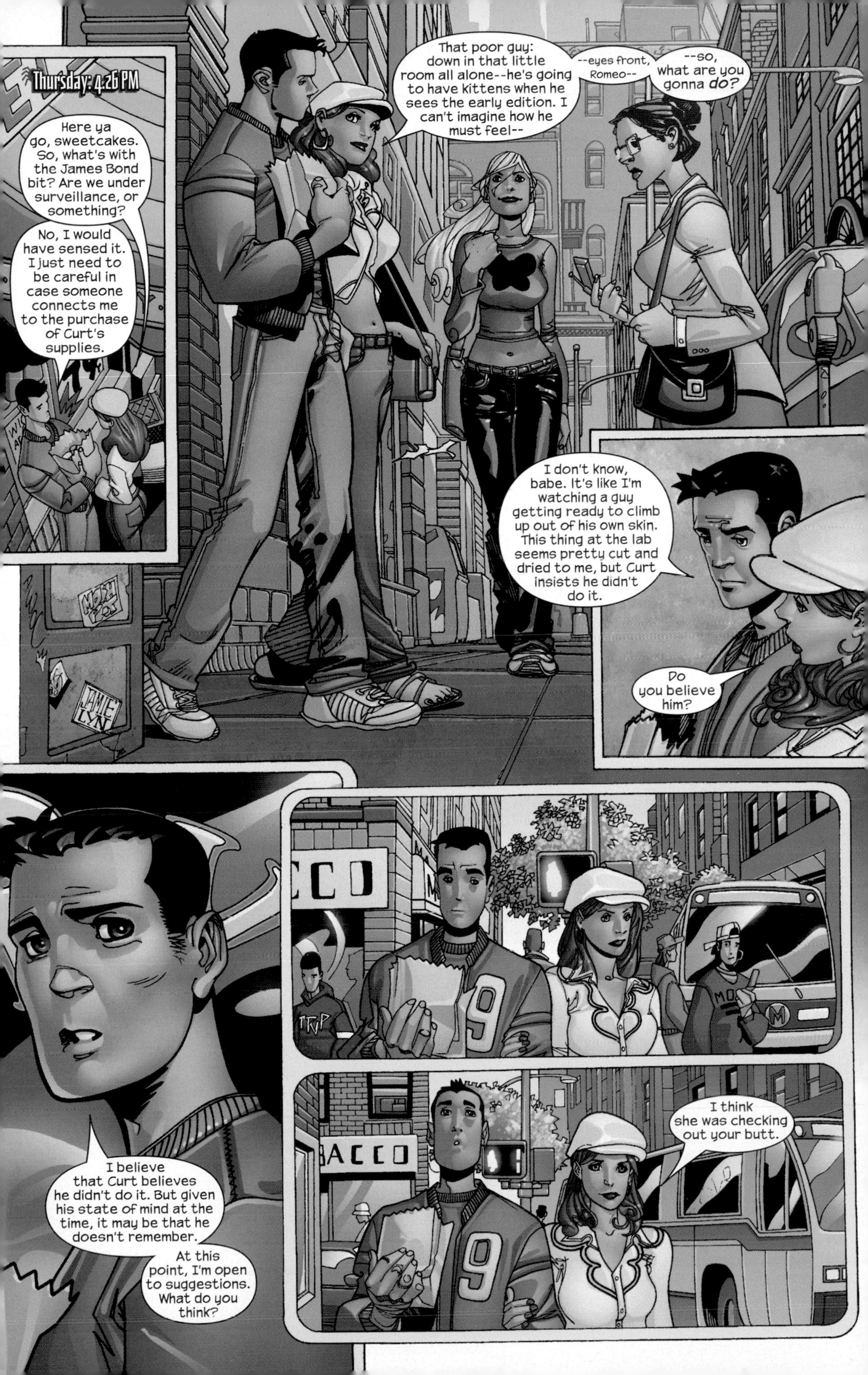
Thursday: 4:26 PM
Here ya go, sweetcakes. So, what's with the James Bond bit? Are we under surveillance, or something?
No, I would have sensed it. I just need to be careful in case someone connects me to the purchase of Curt's supplies.
That poor guy: down in that little room all alone--he's going to have kittens when he sees the early edition. I can't imagine how he must feel--
--eyes front, Romeo--
--so, what are you gonna *do?*
I don't know, babe. It's like I'm watching a guy getting ready to climb up out of his own skin. This thing at the lab seems pretty cut and dried to me, but Curt insists he didn't do it.
Do you believe him?
I believe that Curt believes he didn't do it. But given his state of mind at the time, it may be that he doesn't remember.
At this point, I'm open to suggestions. What do you think?
I think she was checking out your butt.

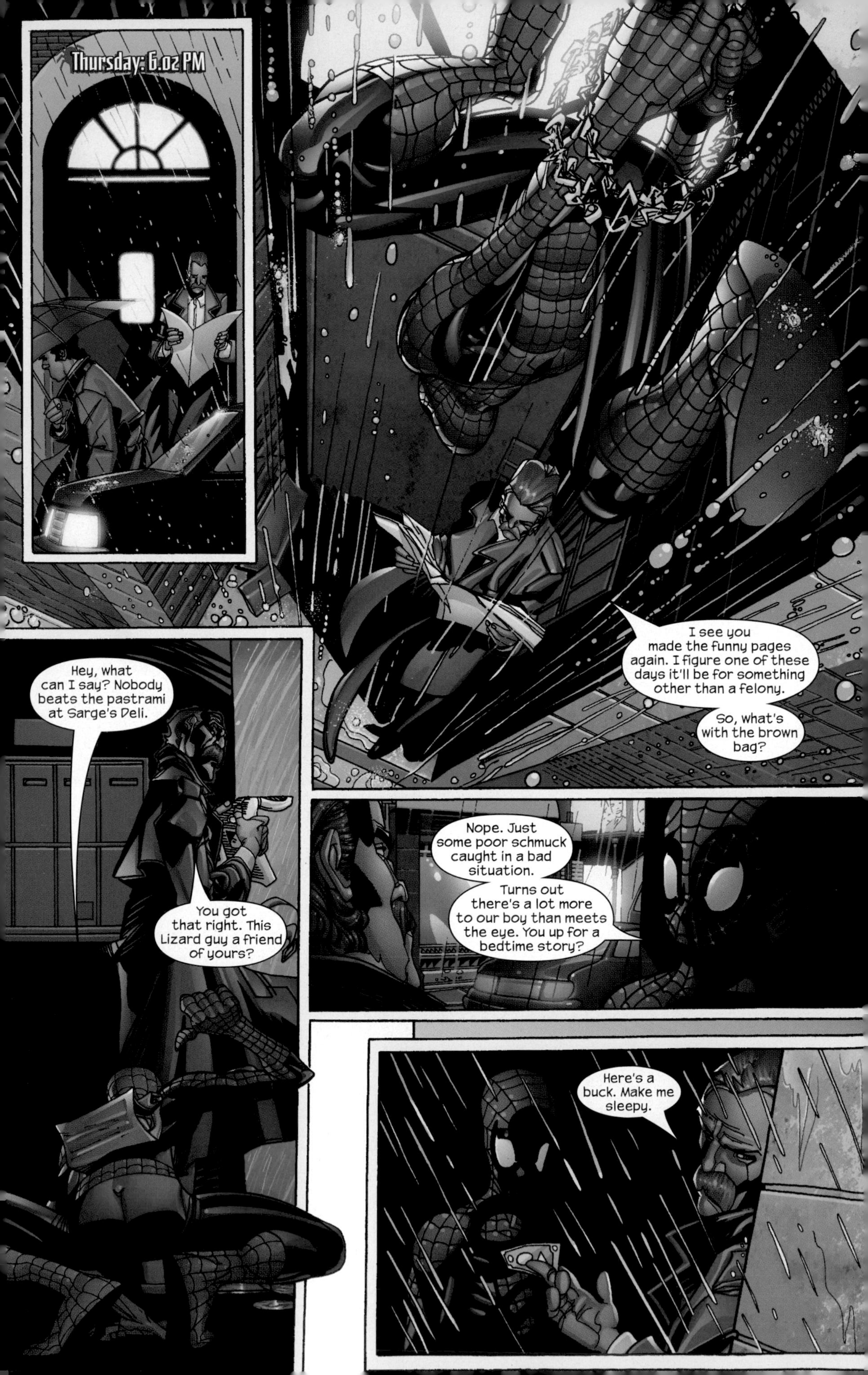
Thursday: 6:02 PM
I see you made the funny pages again. I figure one of these days it'll be for something other than a felony.
So, what's with the brown bag?
Hey, what can I say? Nobody beats the pastrami at Sarge's Deli.
You got that right. This Lizard guy a friend of yours?
Nope. Just some poor schmuck caught in a bad situation.
Turns out there's a lot more to our boy than meets the eye. You up for a bedtime story?
Here's a buck. Make me sleepy.

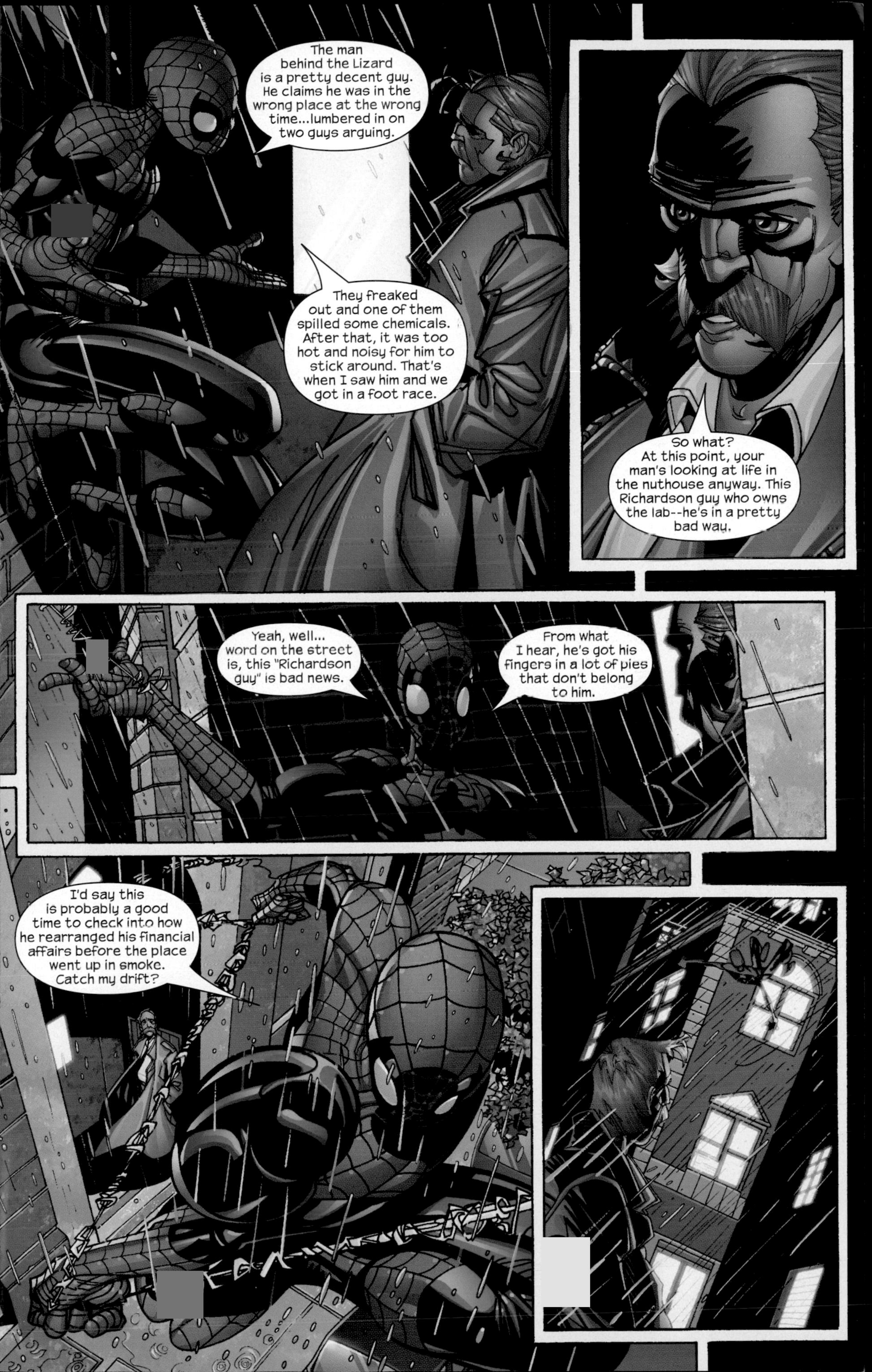
The man behind the Lizard is a pretty decent guy. He claims he was in the wrong place at the wrong time...lumbered in on two guys arguing.
They freaked out and one of them spilled some chemicals. After that, it was too hot and noisy for him to stick around. That's when I saw him and we got in a foot race.
So what? At this point, your man's looking at life in the nuthouse anyway. This Richardson guy who owns the lab--he's in a pretty bad way.
Yeah, well... word on the street is, this "Richardson guy" is bad news.
From what I hear, he's got his fingers in a lot of pies that don't belong to him.
I'd say this is probably a good time to check into how he rearranged his financial affairs before the place went up in smoke. Catch my drift?

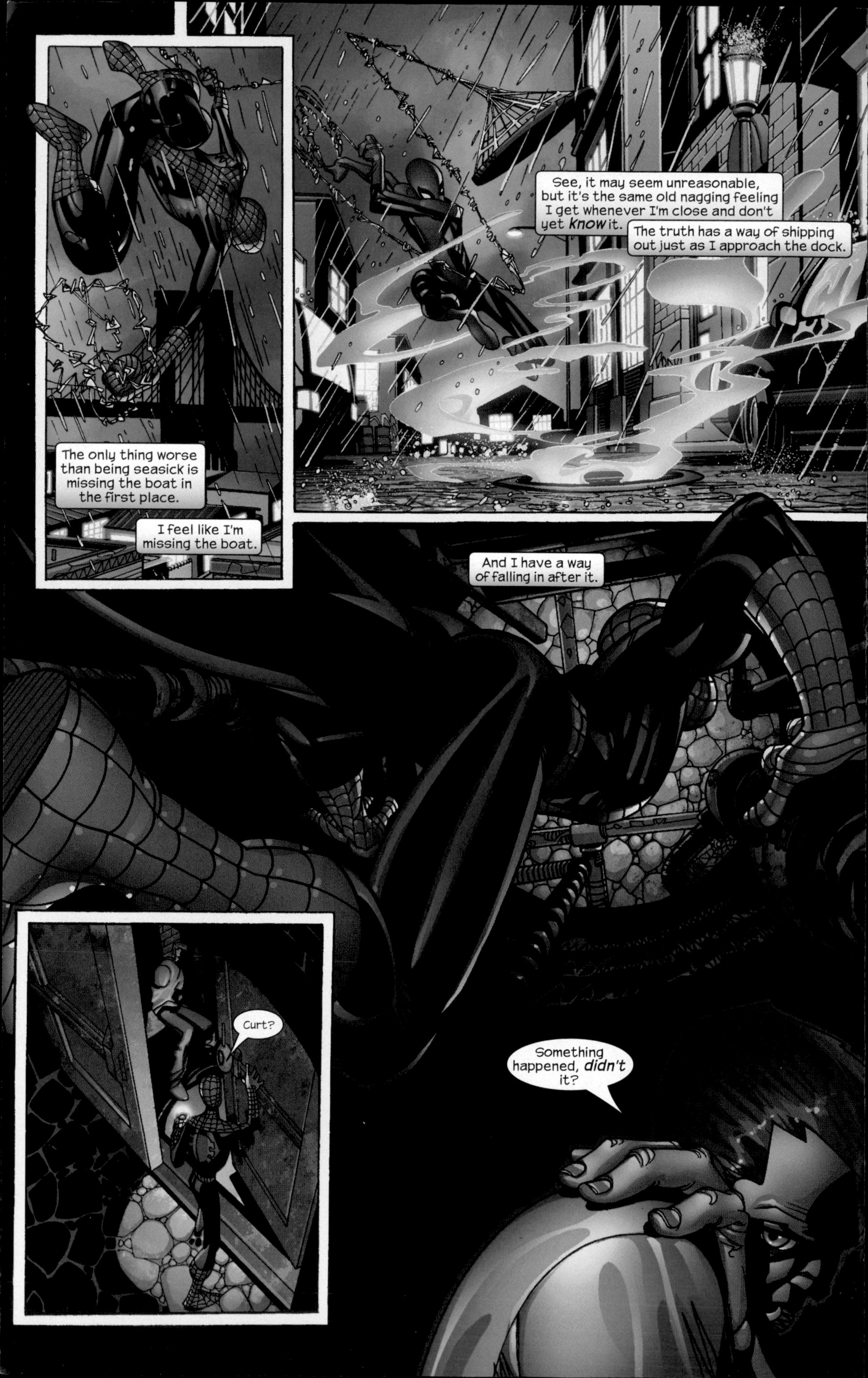
The only thing worse than being seasick is missing the boat in the first place.
I feel like I'm missing the boat.
See, it may seem unreasonable, but it's the same old nagging feeling I get whenever I'm close and don't yet *know* it.
The truth has a way of shipping out just as I approach the dock.
And I have a way of falling in after it.
Curt?
Something happened, *didn't* it?

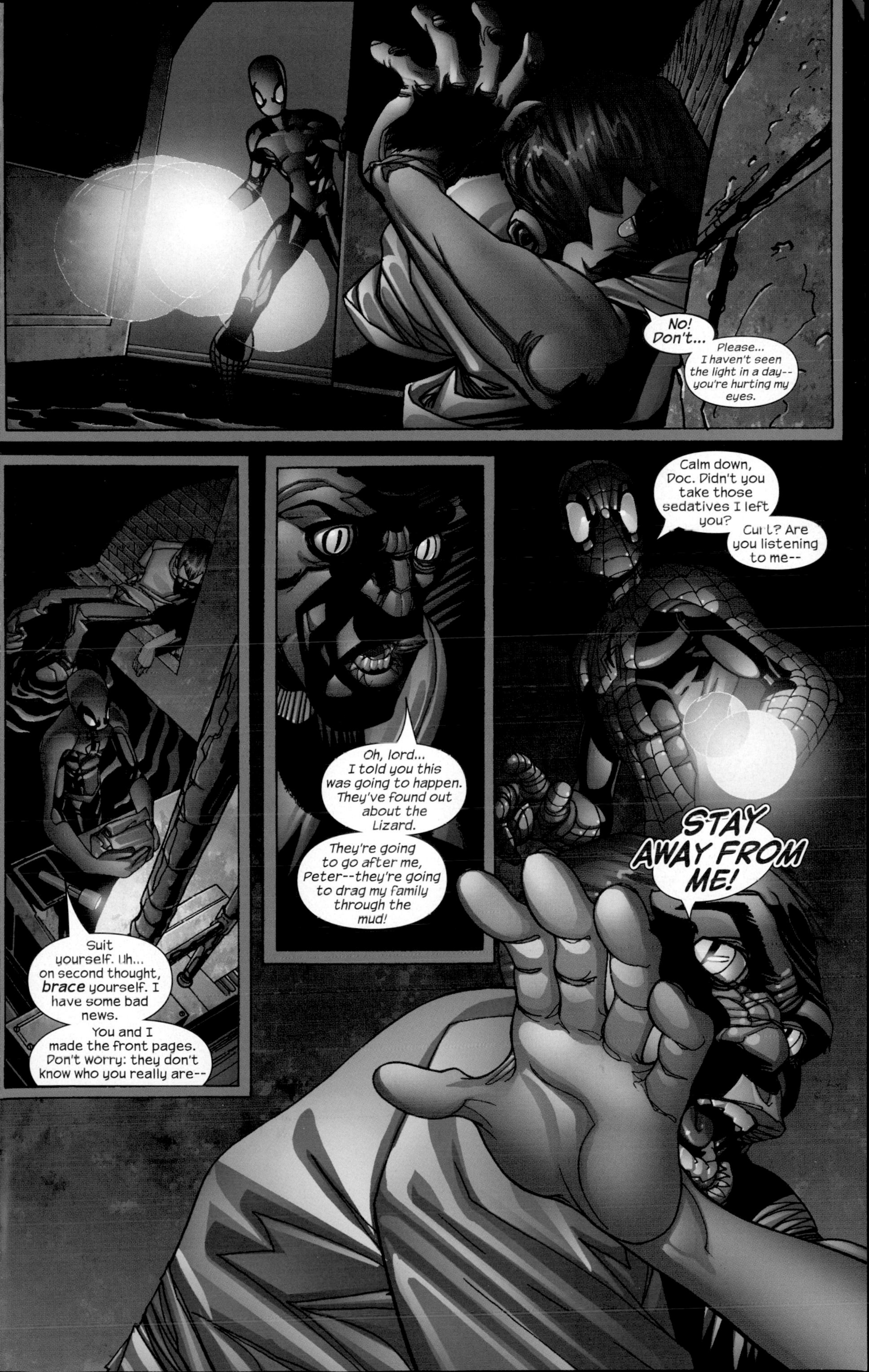

No! Don't...
Please... I haven't seen the light in a day-- you're hurting my eyes.
Calm down, Doc. Didn't you take those sedatives I left you?
Curt? Are you listening to me--
Oh, lord... I told you this was going to happen. They've found out about the Lizard.
They're going to go after me, Peter--they're going to drag my family through the mud!
Suit yourself. Uh... on second thought, brace yourself. I have some bad news.
You and I made the front pages. Don't worry: they don't know who you really are--
STAY AWAY FROM ME!

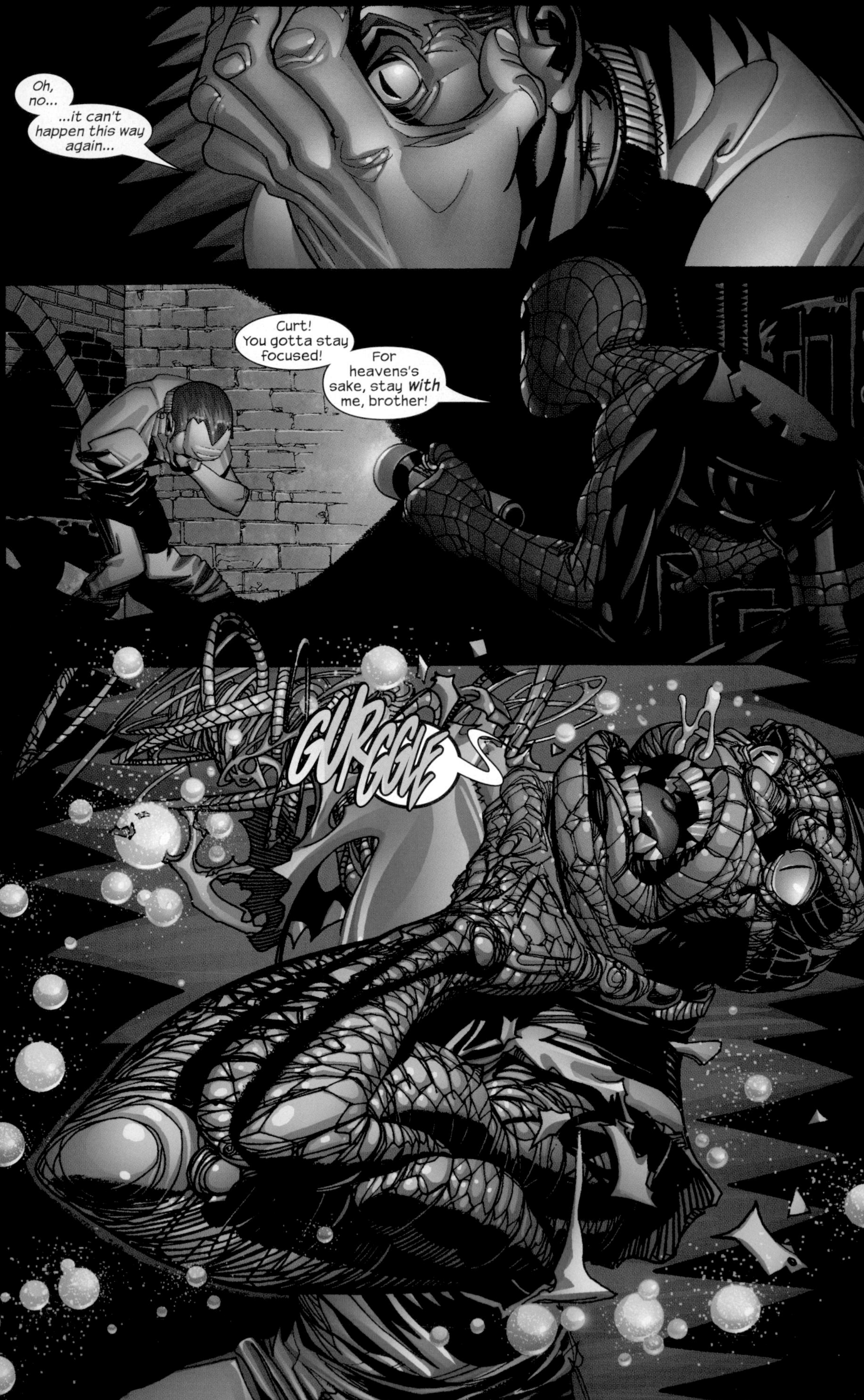
Oh, no... ...it can't happen this way again...
Curt! You gotta stay focused!
For heavens's sake, stay *with* me, brother!
GURGGLE

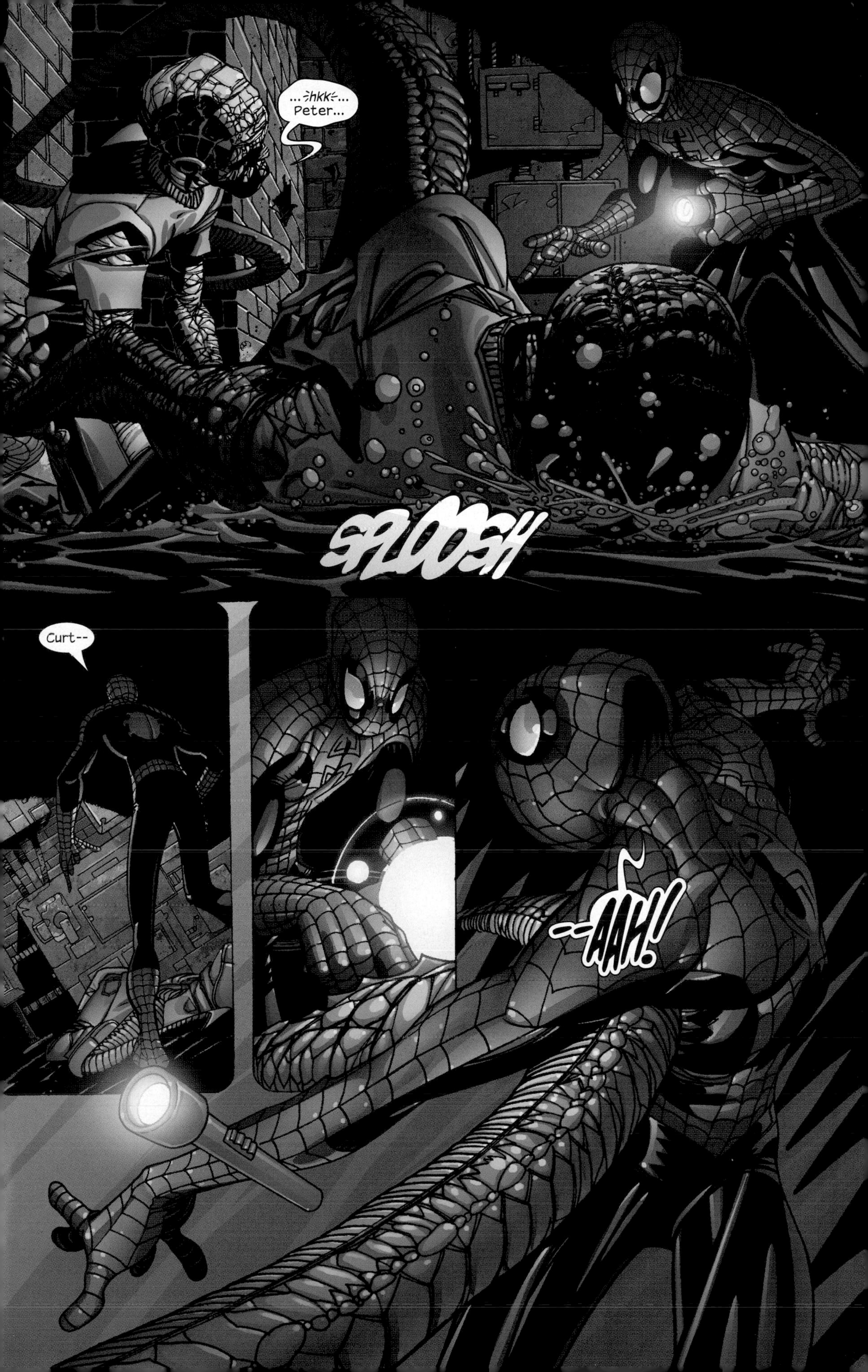
...hkk...
Peter...
SPLOOSH
Curt--
--AAH!

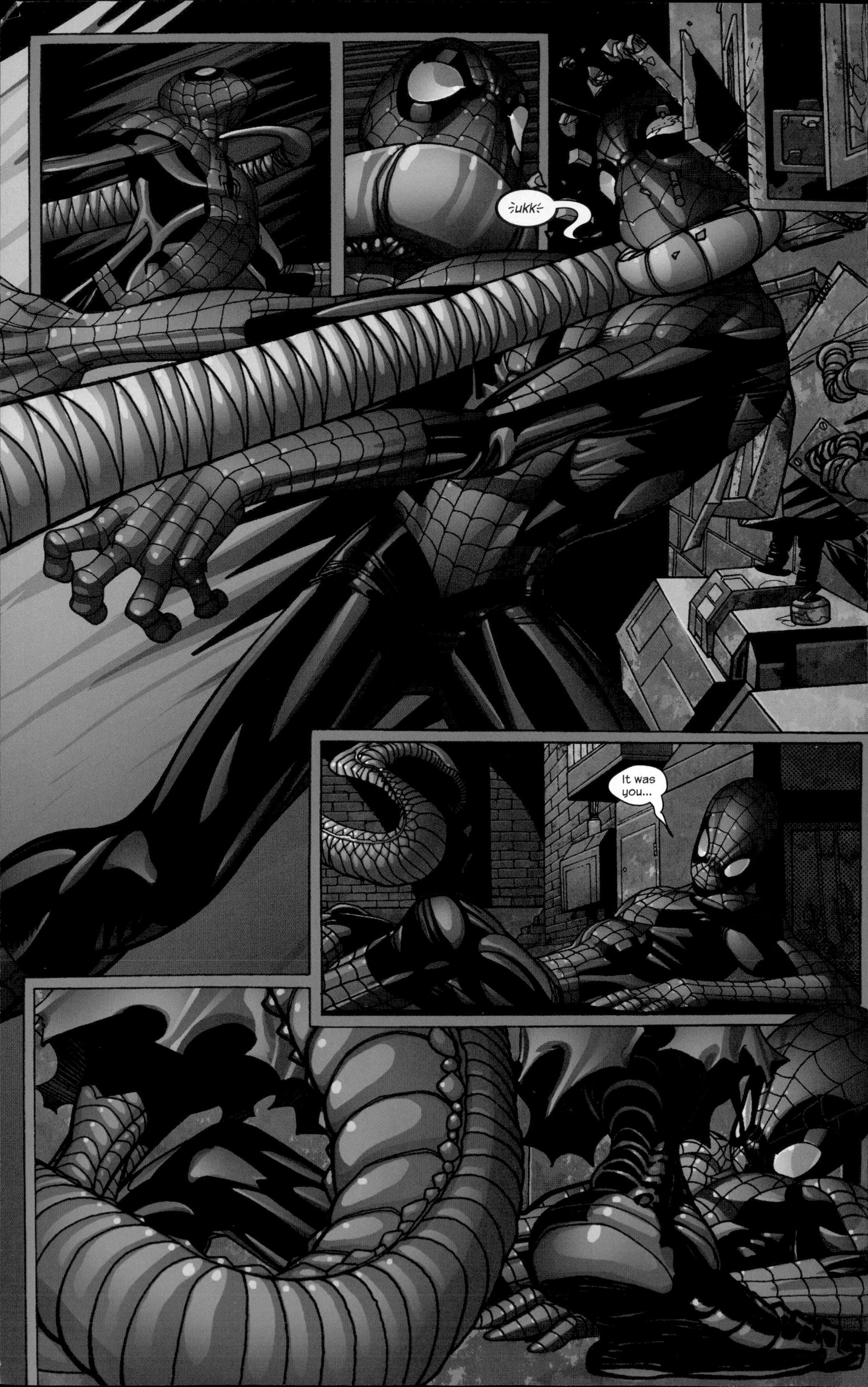
ukk
It was you...

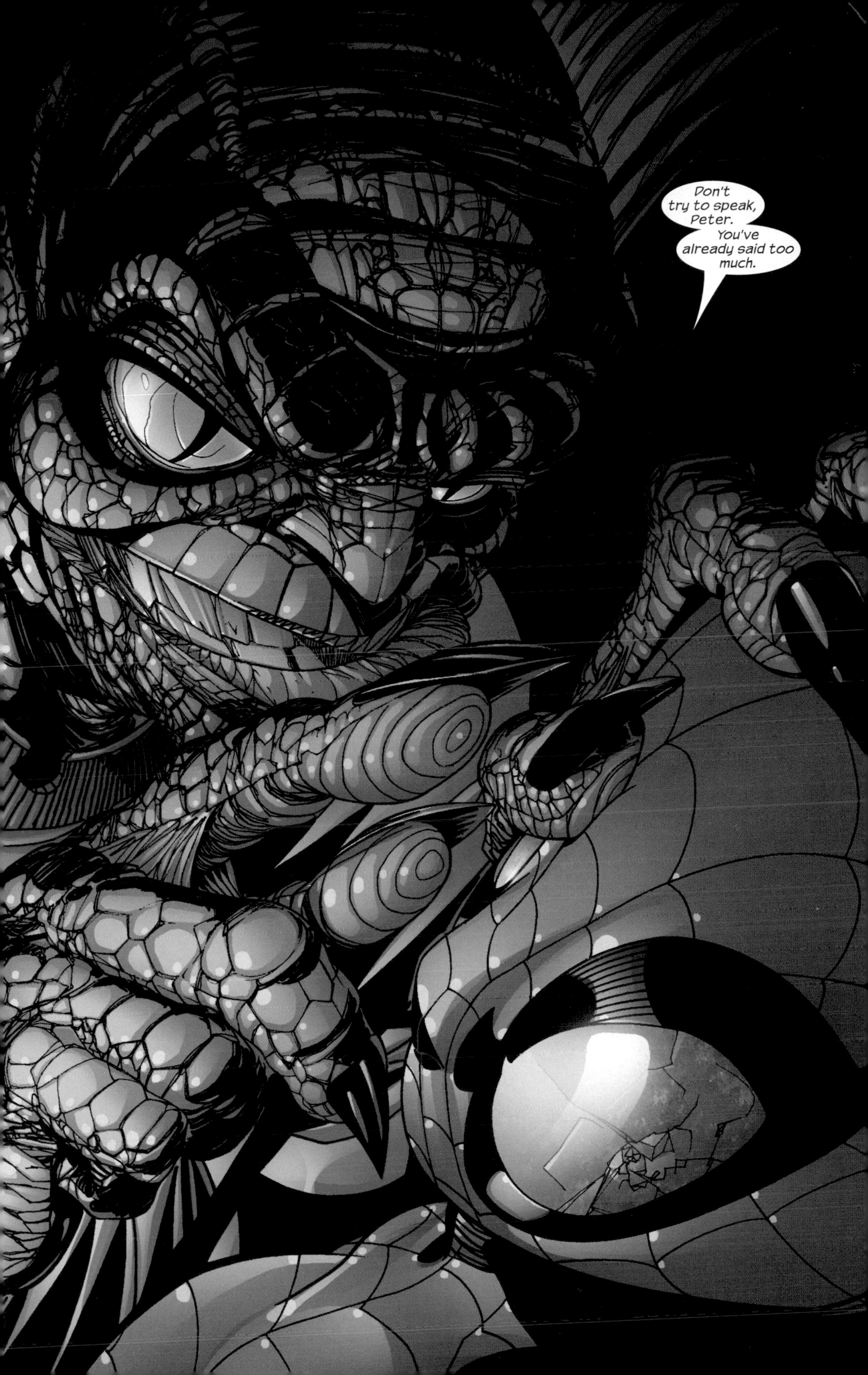
Don't try to speak, Peter.
You've already said too much.

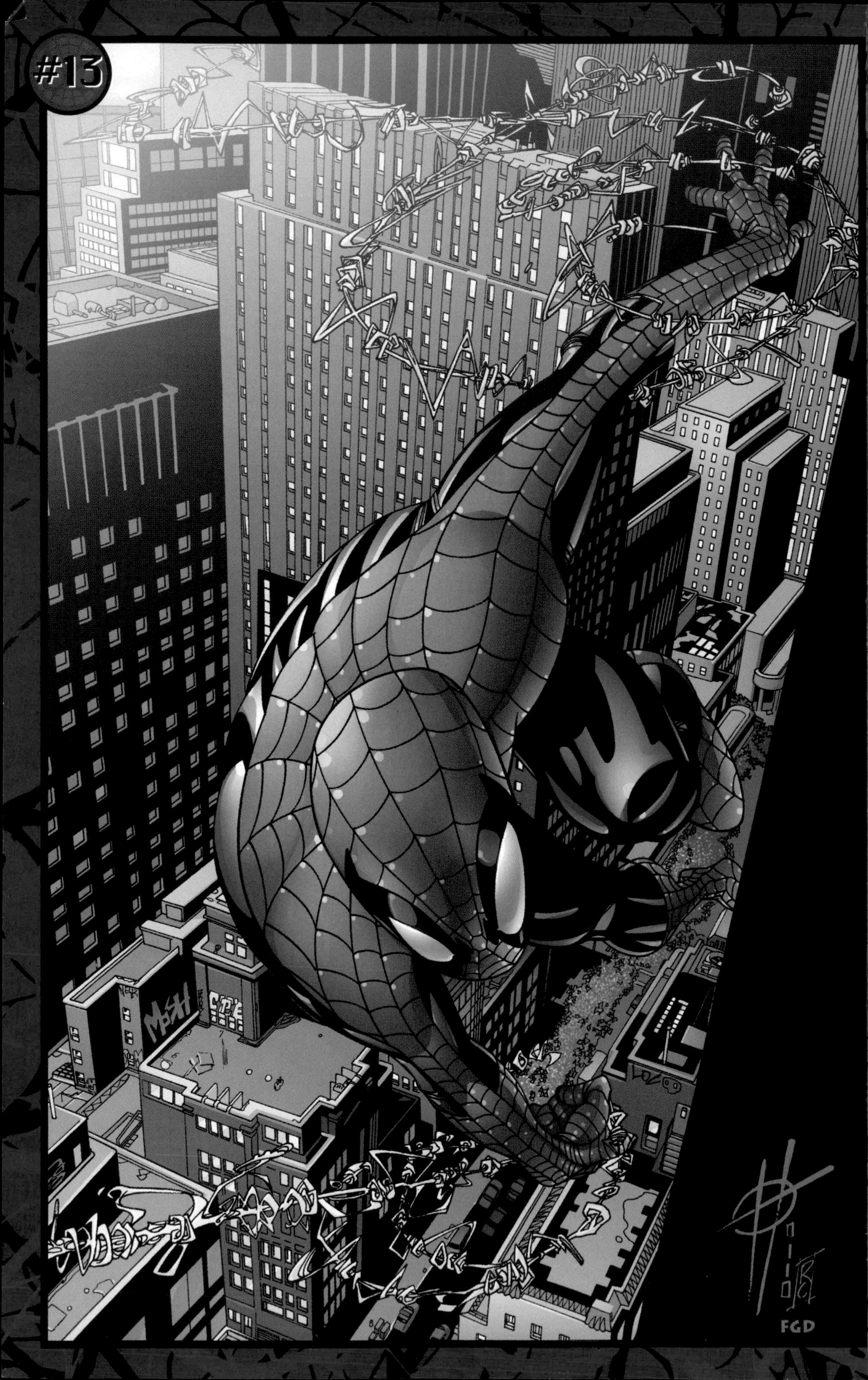
#13
FGD

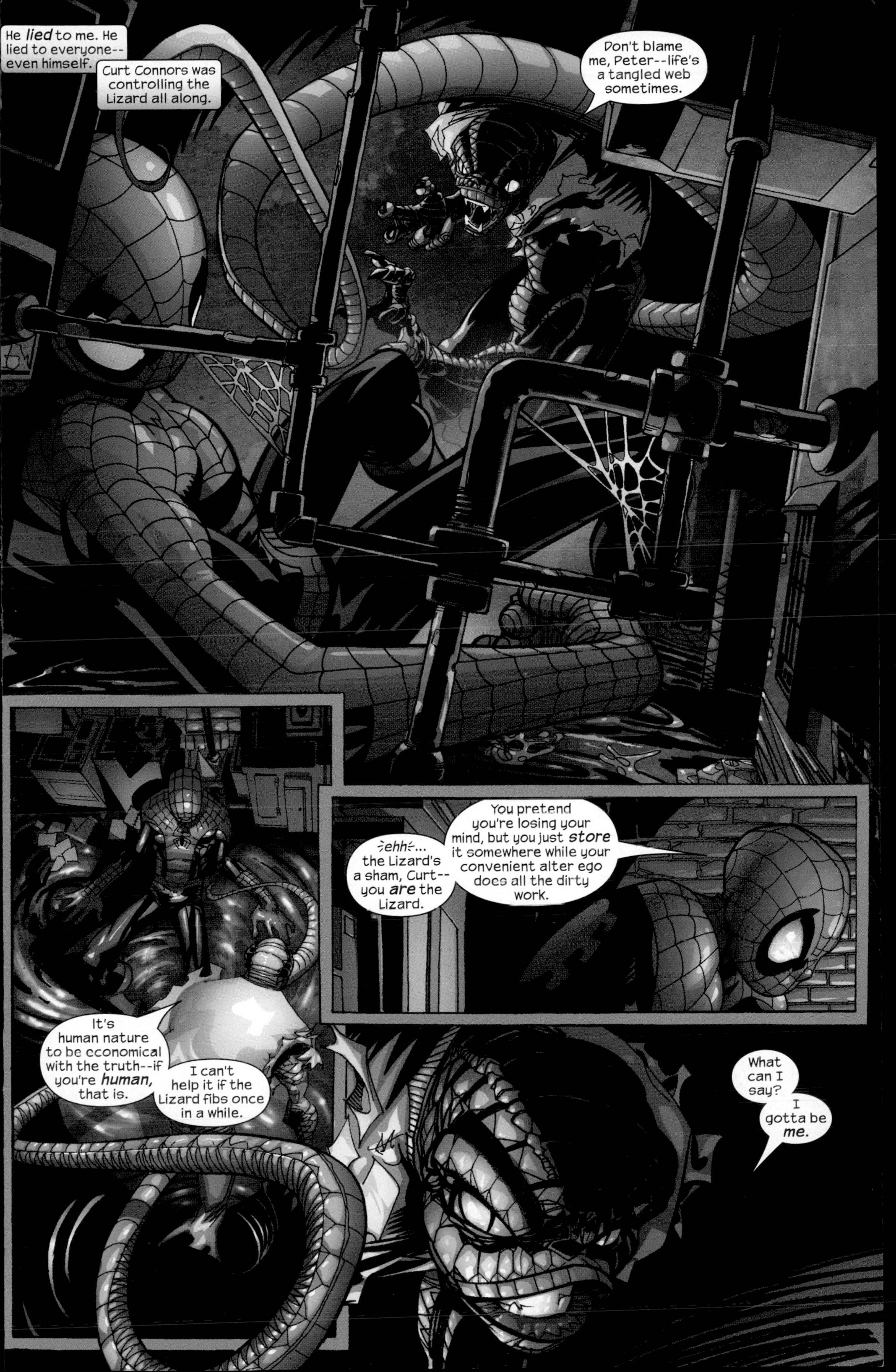
He *lied* to me. He lied to everyone--even himself.
Curt Connors was controlling the Lizard all along.
Don't blame me, Peter--life's a tangled web sometimes.
=ehh=... the Lizard's a sham, Curt--you *are* the Lizard.
You pretend you're losing your mind, but you just *store* it somewhere while your convenient alter ego does all the dirty work.
It's human nature to be economical with the truth--if you're *human,* that is.
I can't help it if the Lizard fibs once in a while.
What can I say?
I gotta be *me.*

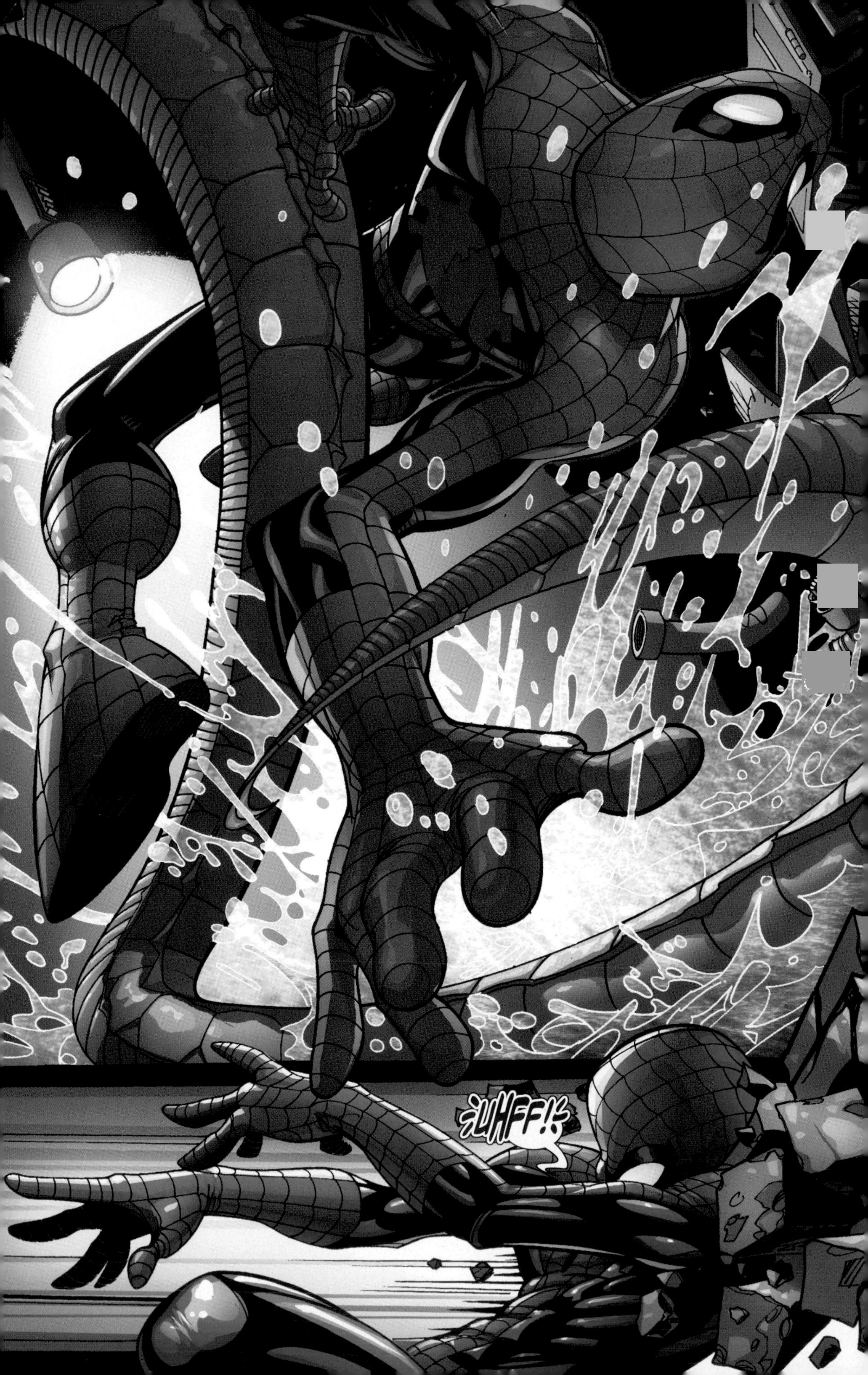
¡UHFF!¡

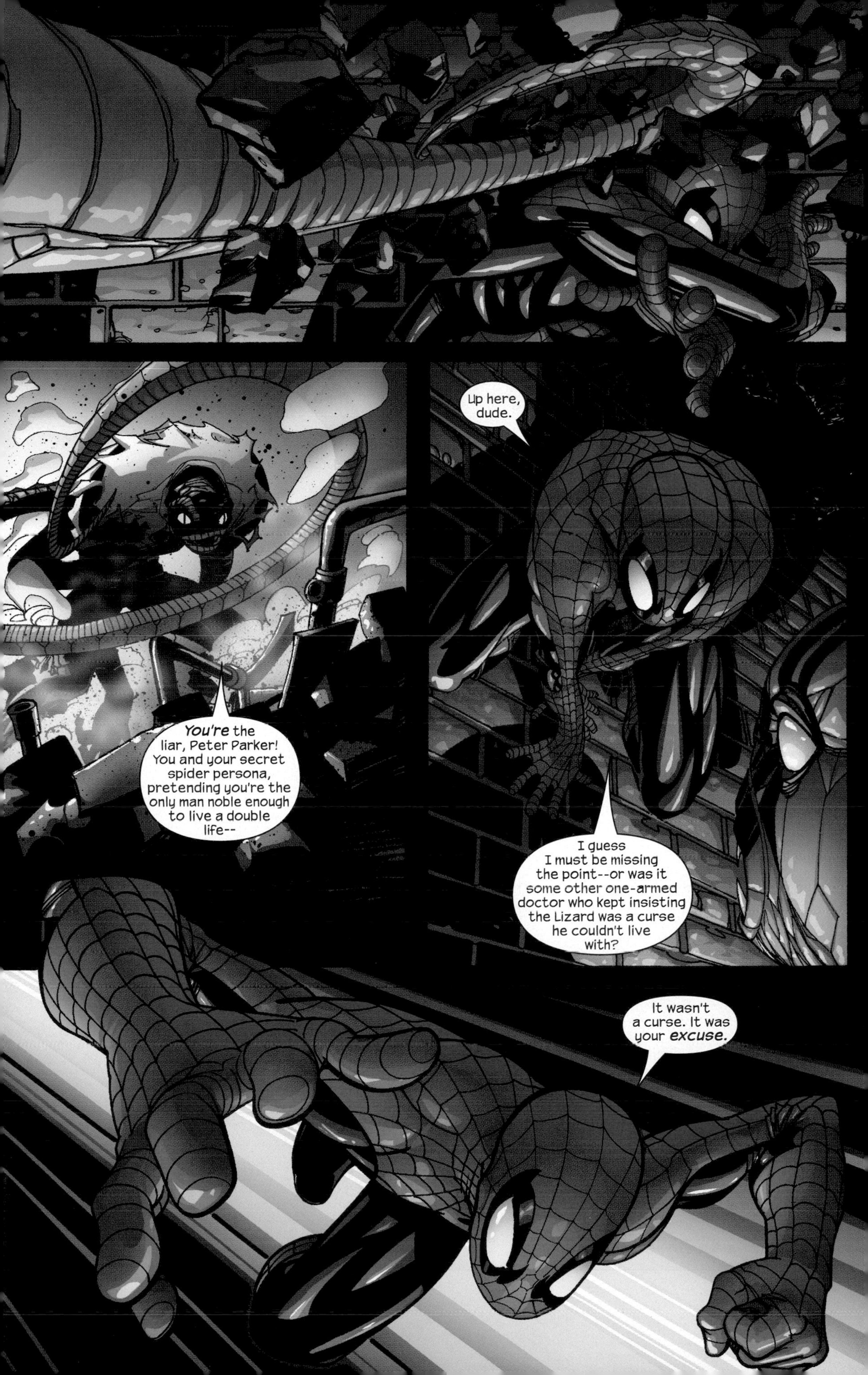

Up here, dude.
You're the liar, Peter Parker! You and your secret spider persona, pretending you're the only man noble enough to live a double life--
I guess I must be missing the point--or was it some other one-armed doctor who kept insisting the Lizard was a curse he couldn't live with?
It wasn't a curse. It was your *excuse.*

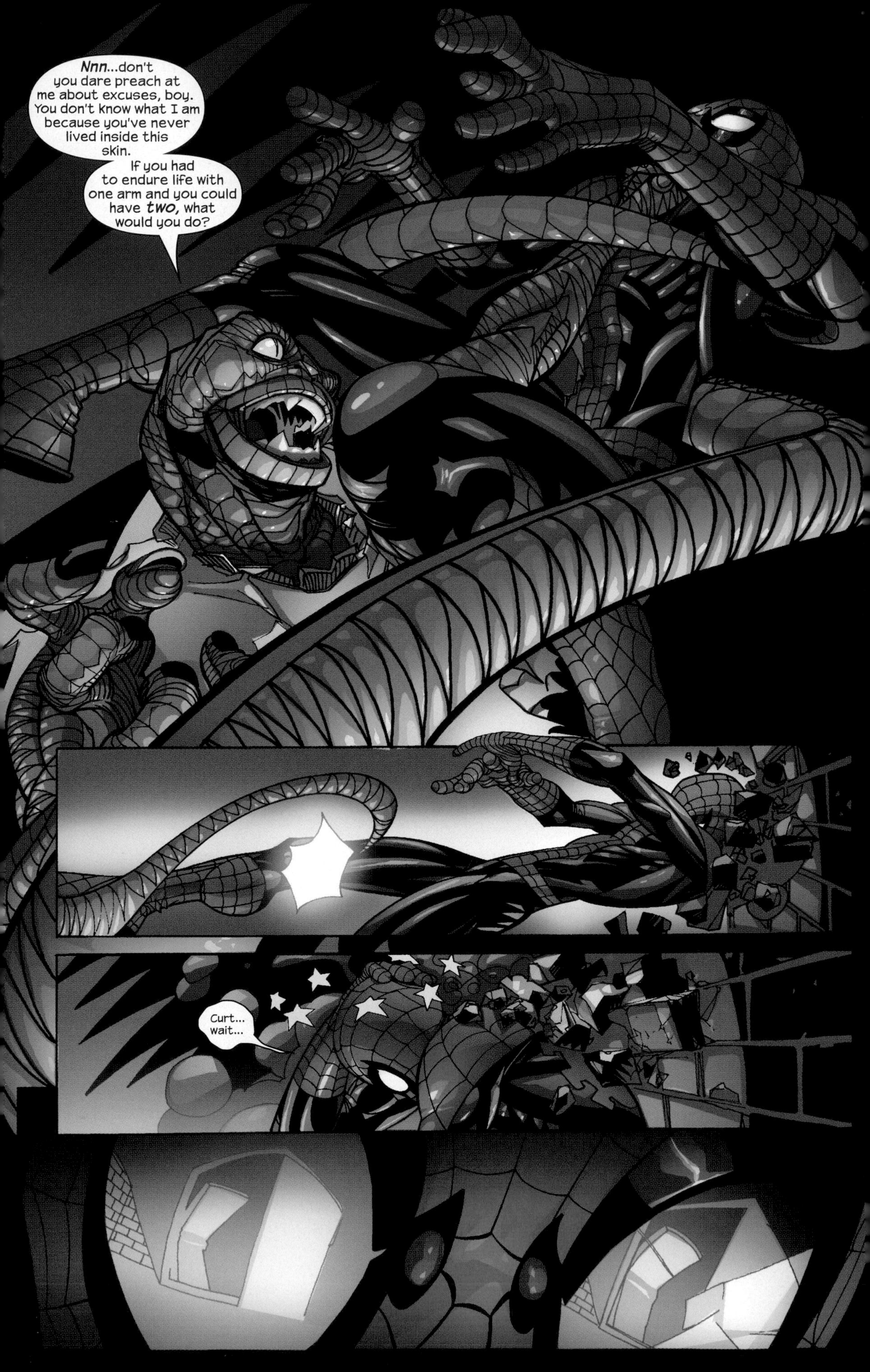
Nnn...don't you dare preach at me about excuses, boy. You don't know what I am because you've never lived inside this skin. If you had to endure life with one arm and you could have two, what would you do?
Curt... wait...

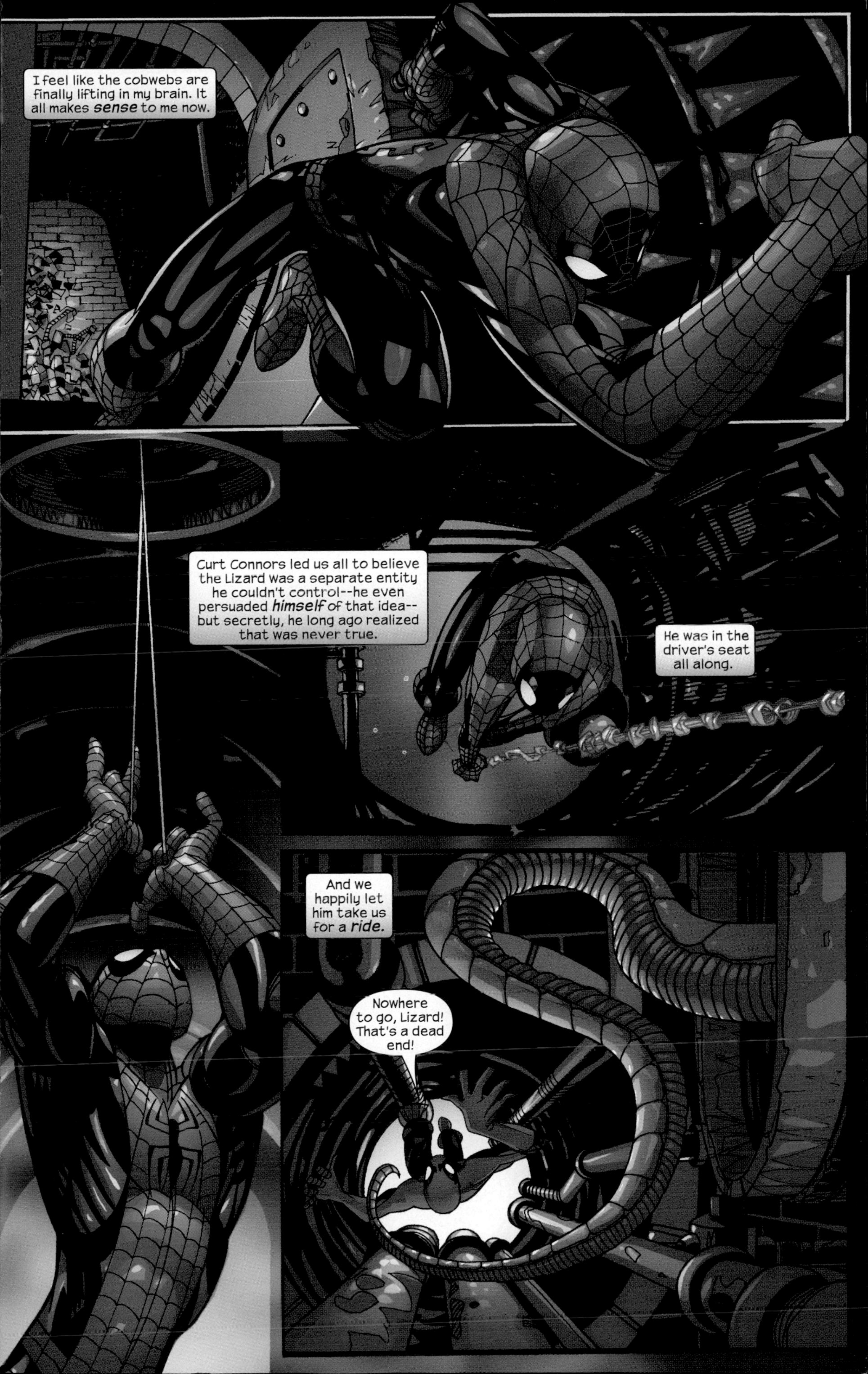
I feel like the cobwebs are finally lifting in my brain. It all makes *sense* to me now.
Curt Connors led us all to believe the Lizard was a separate entity he couldn't control--he even persuaded *himself* of that idea--but secretly, he long ago realized that was never true.
He was in the driver's seat all along.
And we happily let him take us for a *ride.*
Nowhere to go, Lizard! That's a dead end!

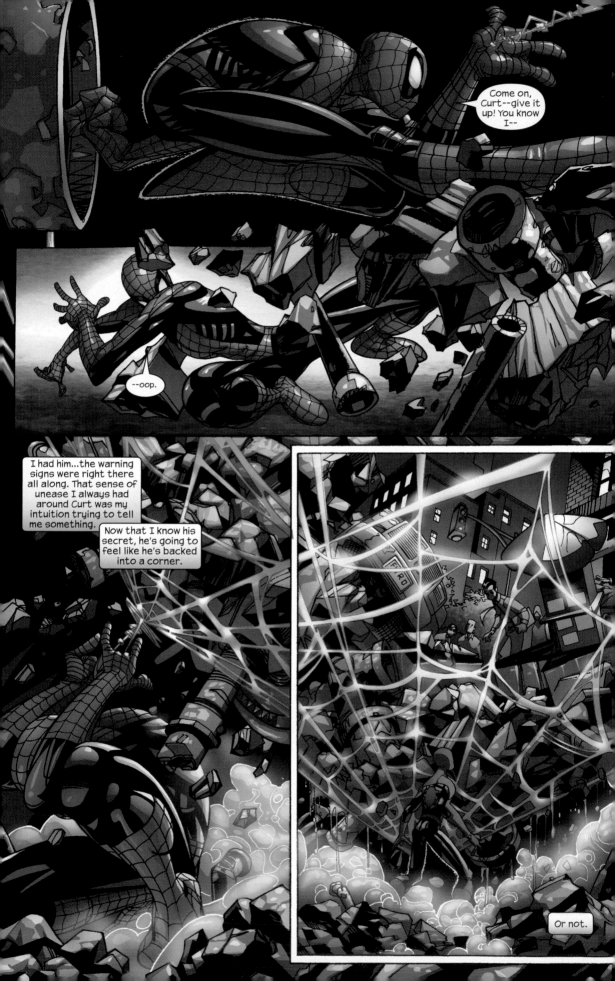

Come on, Curt--give it up! You know I--

--oop.

I had him...the warning signs were right there all along. That sense of unease I always had around Curt was my intuition trying to tell me something.

Now that I know his secret, he's going to feel like he's backed into a corner.

Or not.

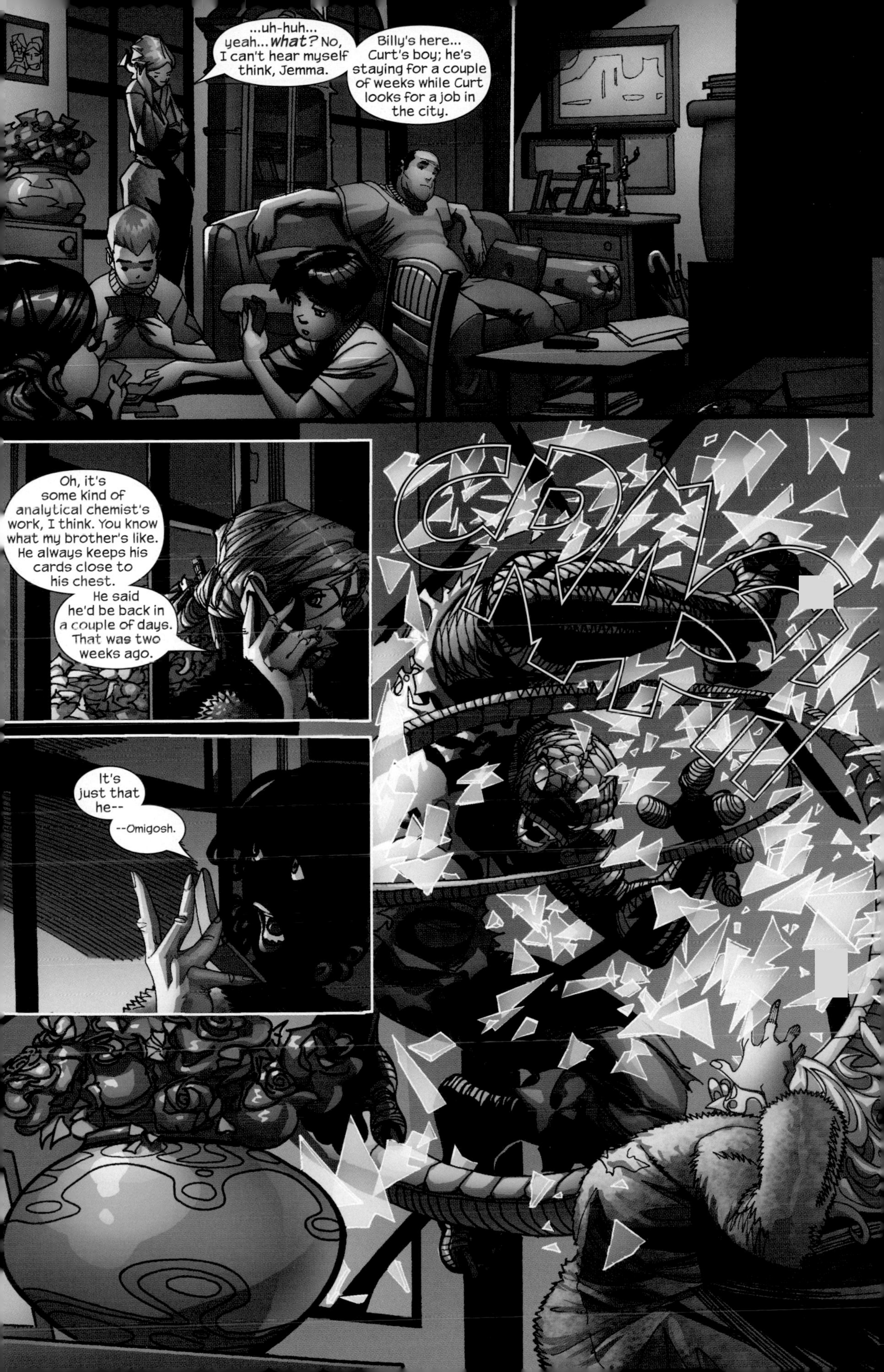

...uh-huh... yeah...what? No, I can't hear myself think, Jemma.
Billy's here... Curt's boy; he's staying for a couple of weeks while Curt looks for a job in the city.
Oh, it's some kind of analytical chemist's work, I think. You know what my brother's like. He always keeps his cards close to his chest.
He said he'd be back in a couple of days. That was two weeks ago.
It's just that he--
--Omigosh.
CRASH

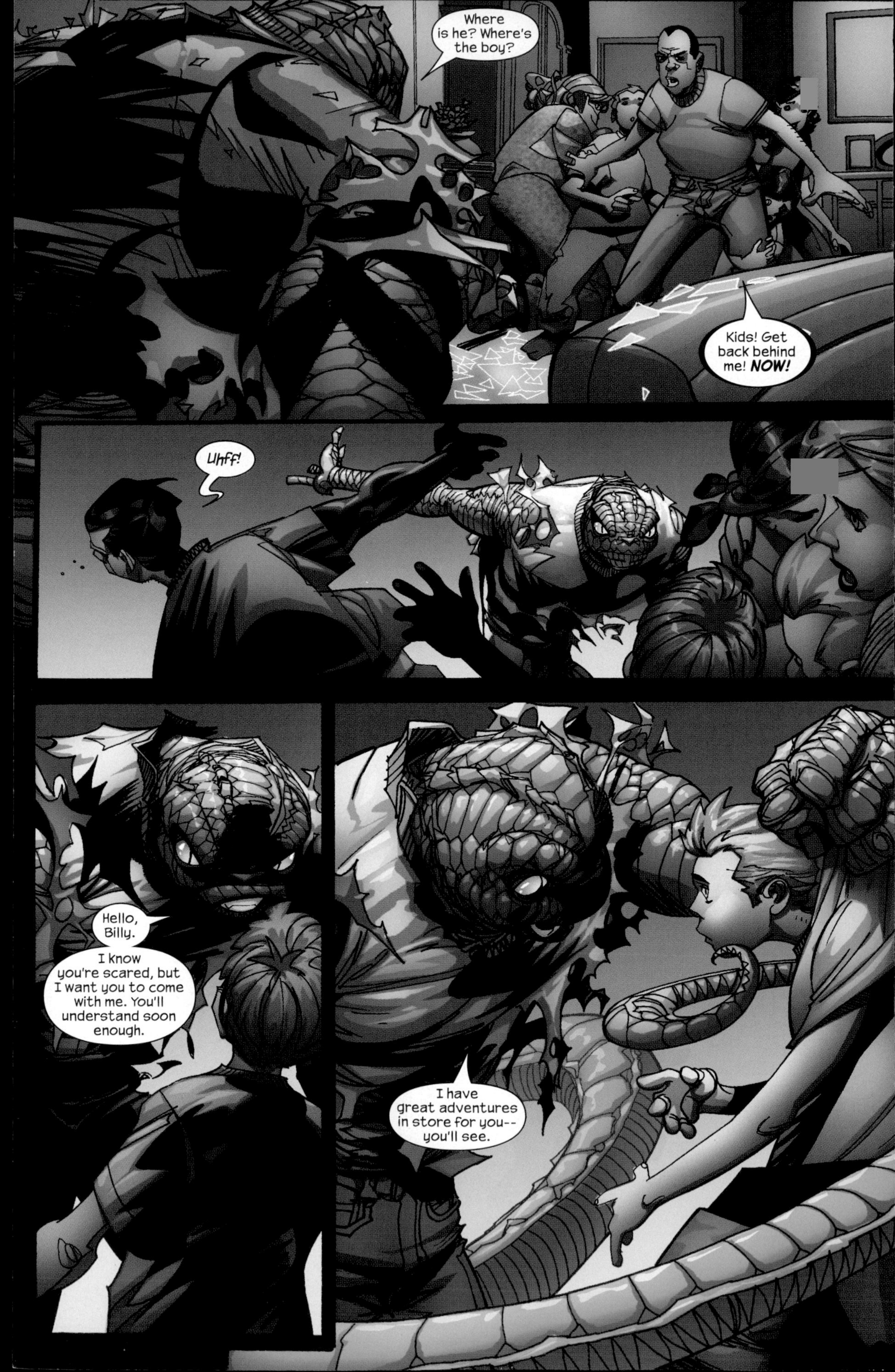

Where is he? Where's the boy?
Kids! Get back behind me! NOW!
Uhff!
Hello, Billy.
I know you're scared, but I want you to come with me. You'll understand soon enough.
I have great adventures in store for you-- you'll see.

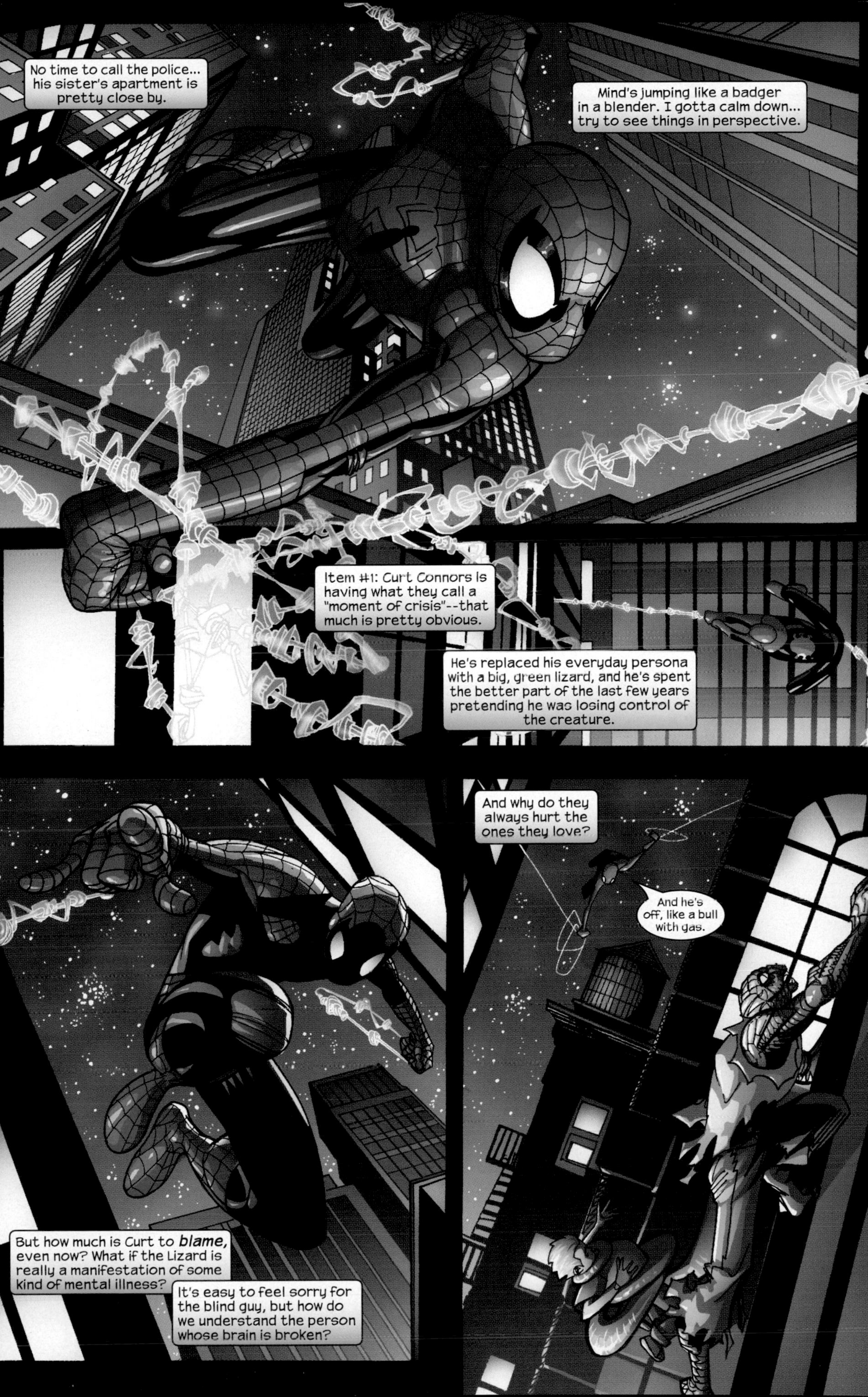
No time to call the police... his sister's apartment is pretty close by.
Mind's jumping like a badger in a blender. I gotta calm down... try to see things in perspective.
Item #1: Curt Connors is having what they call a "moment of crisis"--that much is pretty obvious.
He's replaced his everyday persona with a big, green lizard, and he's spent the better part of the last few years pretending he was losing control of the creature.
But how much is Curt to *blame,* even now? What if the Lizard is really a manifestation of some kind of mental illness?
It's easy to feel sorry for the blind guy, but how do we understand the person whose brain is broken?
And why do they always hurt the ones they love?
And he's off, like a bull with gas.

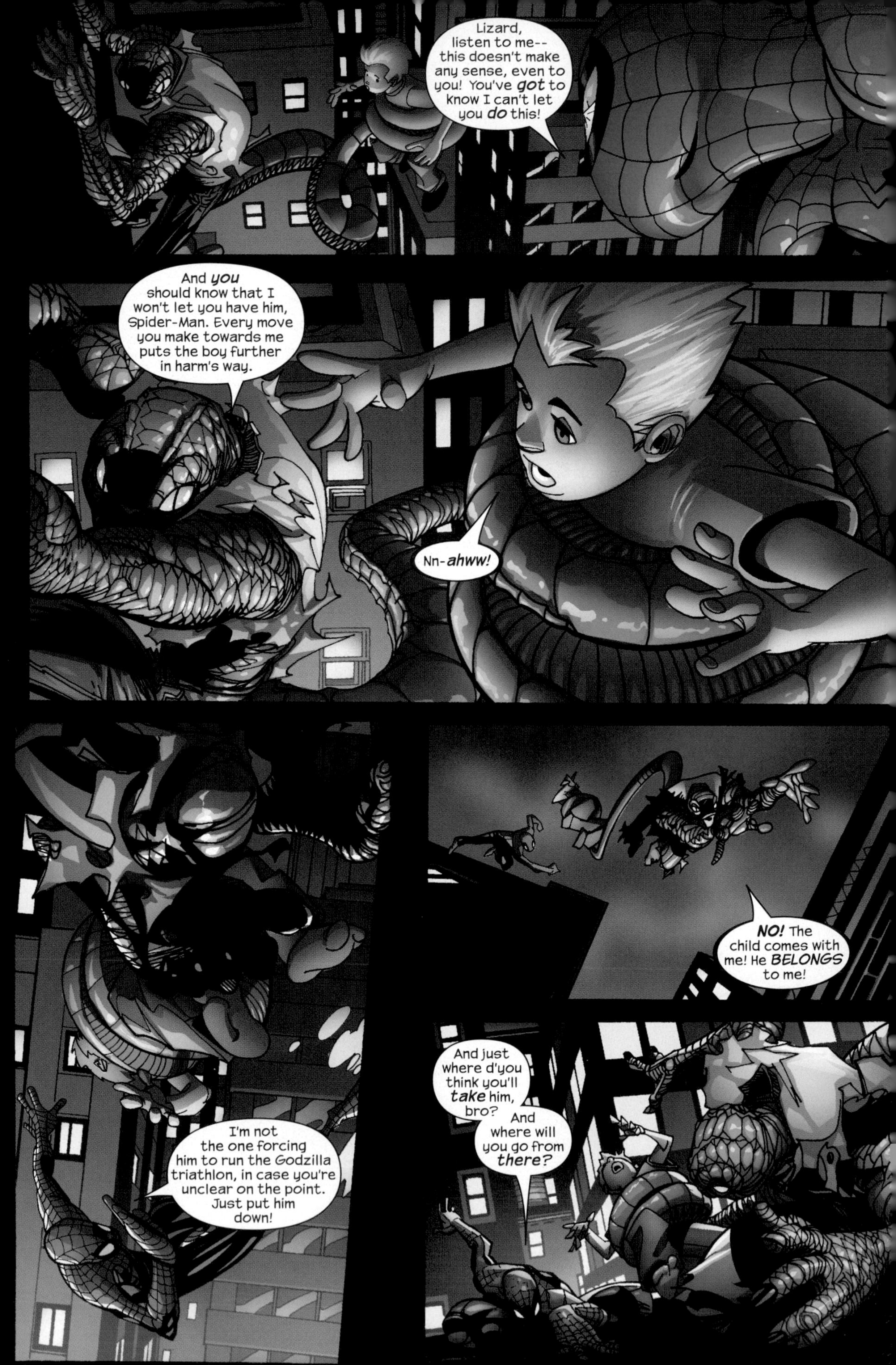
Lizard, listen to me-- this doesn't make any sense, even to you! You've *got* to know I can't let you *do* this!
And *you* should know that I won't let you have him, Spider-Man. Every move you make towards me puts the boy further in harm's way.
Nn-*ahww!*
I'm not the one forcing him to run the Godzilla triathlon, in case you're unclear on the point. Just put him down!
NO! The child comes with me! He *BELONGS* to me!
And just where d'you think you'll *take* him, bro?
And where will you go from *there?*

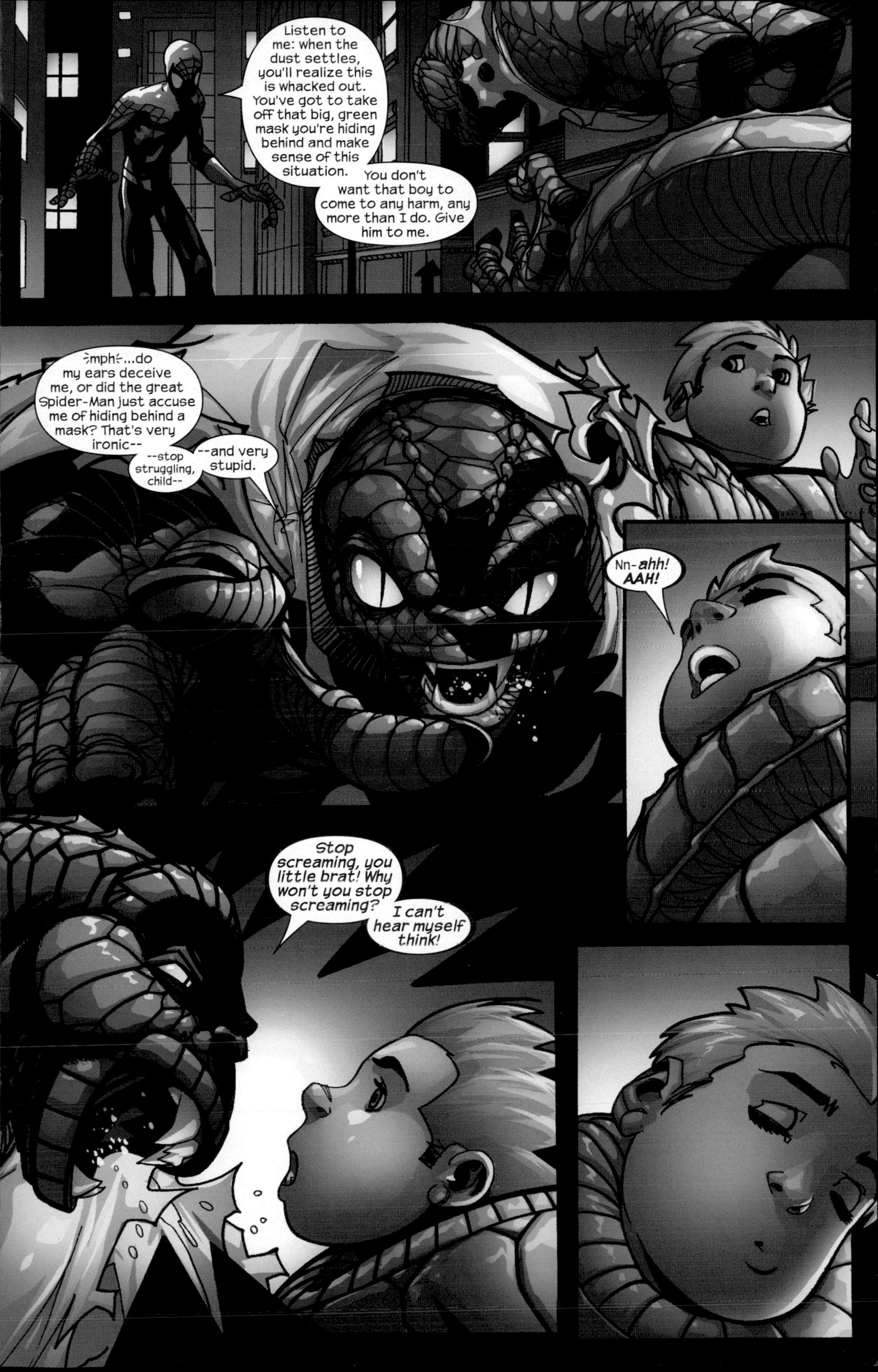
Listen to me: when the dust settles, you'll realize this is whacked out. You've got to take off that big, green mask you're hiding behind and make sense of this situation.
You don't want that boy to come to any harm, any more than I do. Give him to me.
Hmph...do my ears deceive me, or did the great Spider-Man just accuse me of hiding behind a mask? That's very ironic--
--stop struggling, child--
--and very stupid.
Nn-ahh! AAH!
Stop screaming, you little brat! Why won't you stop screaming?
I can't hear myself think!

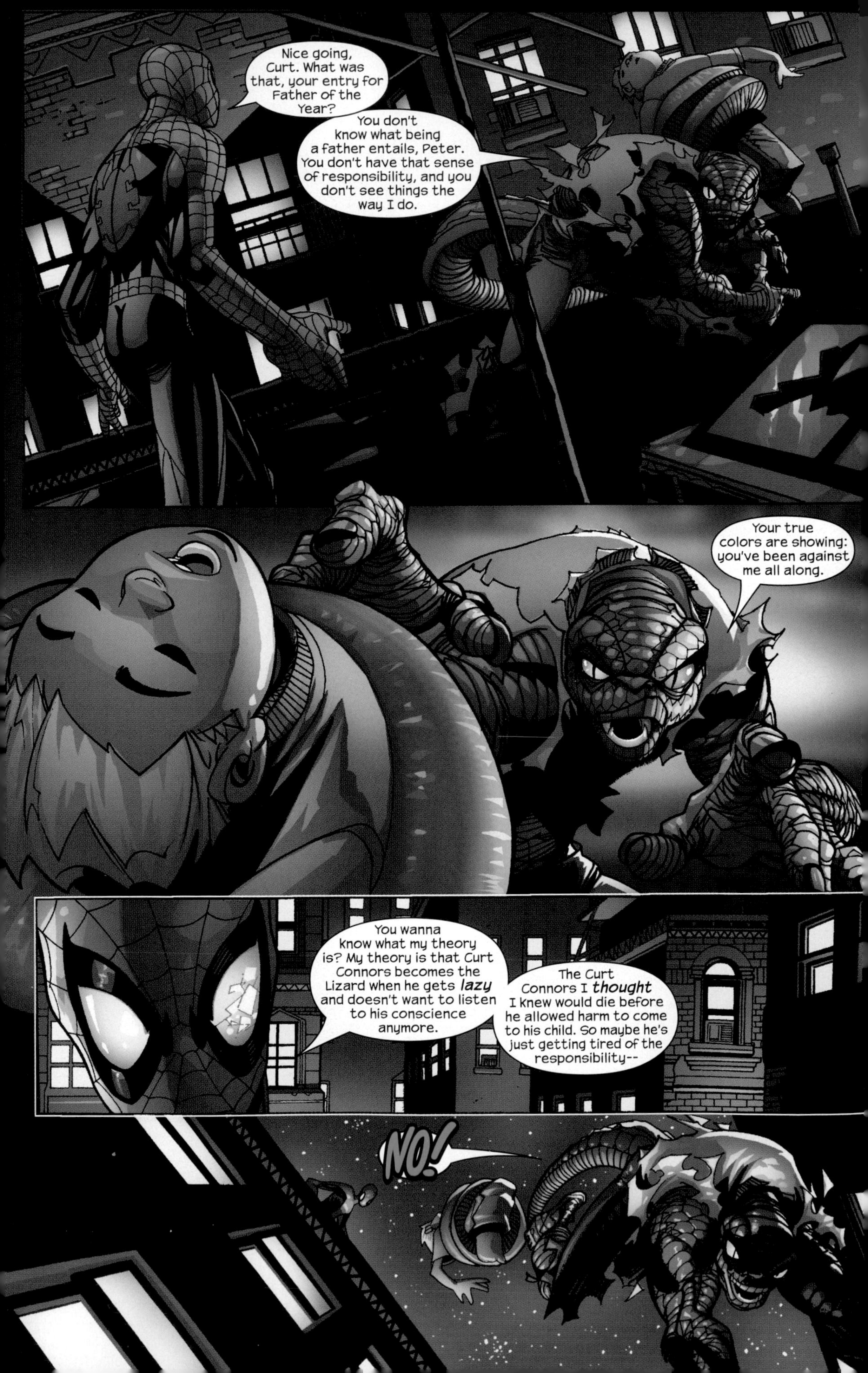
Nice going, Curt. What was that, your entry for Father of the Year?
You don't know what being a father entails, Peter. You don't have that sense of responsibility, and you don't see things the way I do.
Your true colors are showing: you've been against me all along.
You wanna know what my theory is? My theory is that Curt Connors becomes the Lizard when he gets *lazy* and doesn't want to listen to his conscience anymore.
The Curt Connors I *thought* I knew would die before he allowed harm to come to his child. So maybe he's just getting tired of the responsibility--
NO!

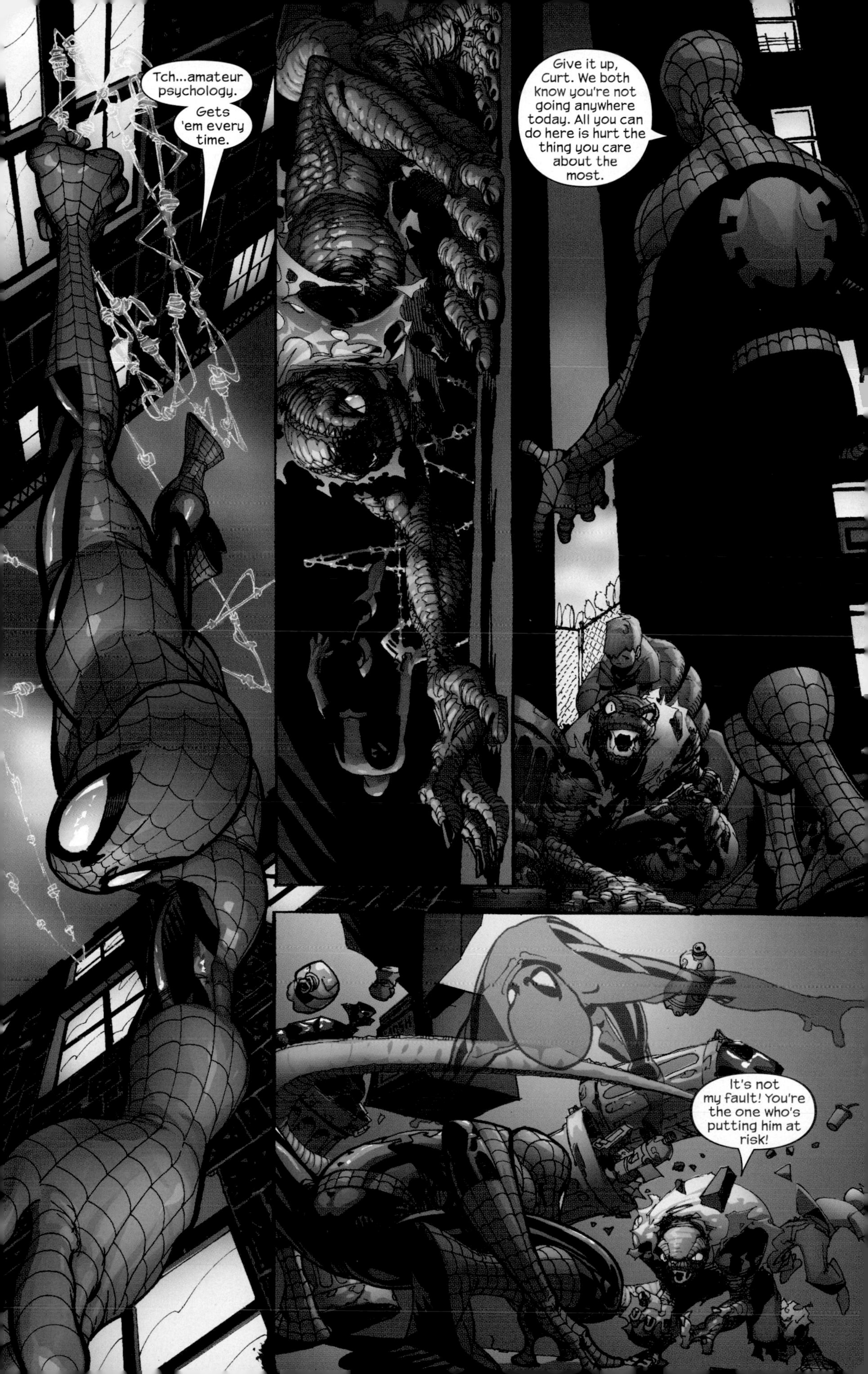
Tch...amateur psychology.
Gets 'em every time.
Give it up, Curt. We both know you're not going anywhere today. All you can do here is hurt the thing you care about the most.
It's not my fault! You're the one who's putting him at risk!

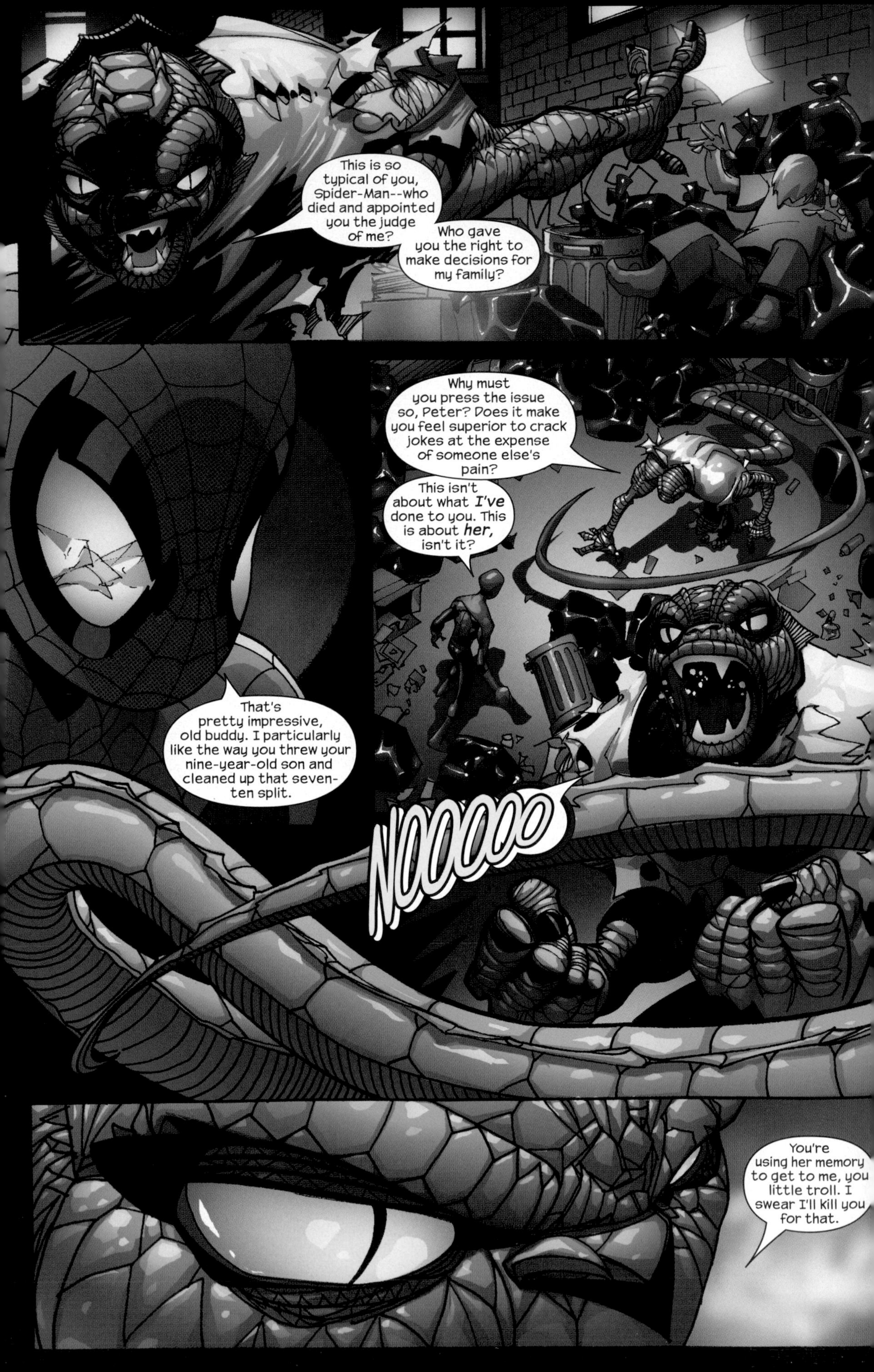
This is so typical of you, Spider-Man--who died and appointed you the judge of me?
Who gave you the right to make decisions for my family?
Why must you press the issue so, Peter? Does it make you feel superior to crack jokes at the expense of someone else's pain?
This isn't about what *I've* done to you. This is about *her,* isn't it?
That's pretty impressive, old buddy. I particularly like the way you threw your nine-year-old son and cleaned up that seven-ten split.
NOOOOO
You're using her memory to get to me, you little troll. I swear I'll kill you for that.

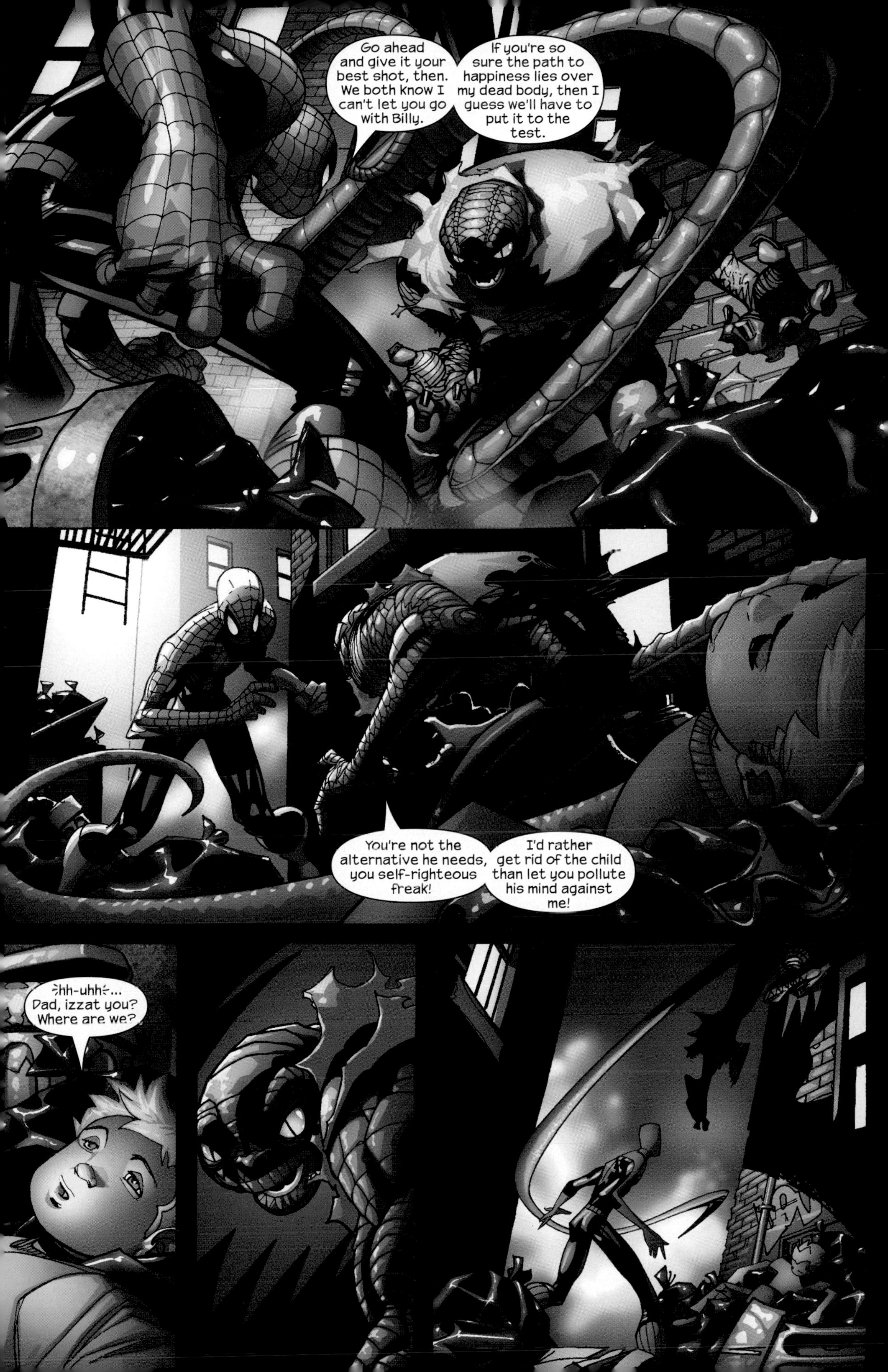

Go ahead and give it your best shot, then. We both know I can't let you go with Billy.
If you're so sure the path to happiness lies over my dead body, then I guess we'll have to put it to the test.
You're not the alternative he needs, you self-righteous freak!
I'd rather get rid of the child than let you pollute his mind against me!
hh-uhh... Dad, izzat you? Where are we?

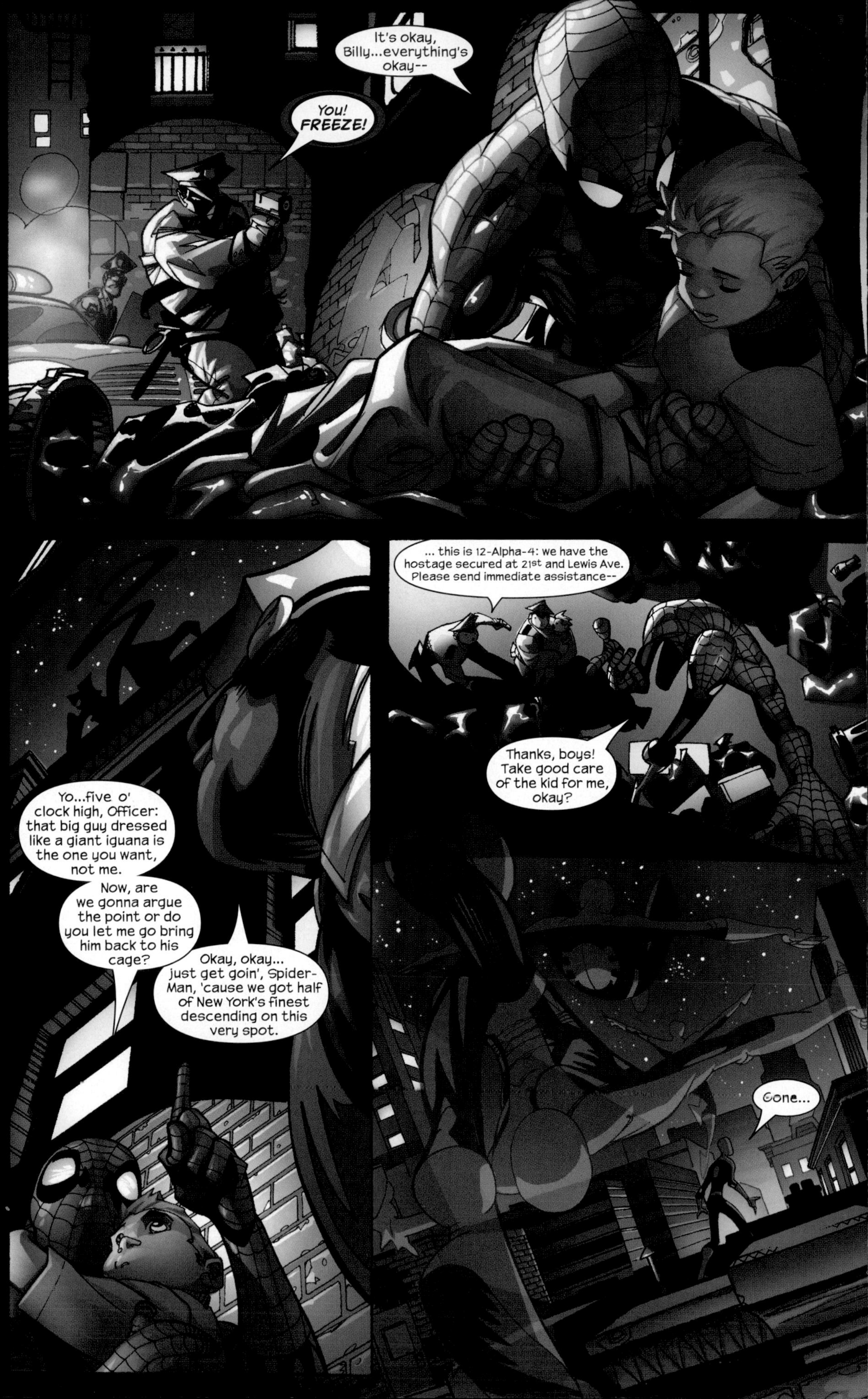
It's okay, Billy...everything's okay--
You! FREEZE!
Yo...five o' clock high, Officer: that big guy dressed like a giant iguana is the one you want, not me.
Now, are we gonna argue the point or do you let me go bring him back to his cage?
Okay, okay... just get goin', Spider-Man, 'cause we got half of New York's finest descending on this very spot.
... this is 12-Alpha-4: we have the hostage secured at 21st and Lewis Ave. Please send immediate assistance--
Thanks, boys! Take good care of the kid for me, okay?
Gone...

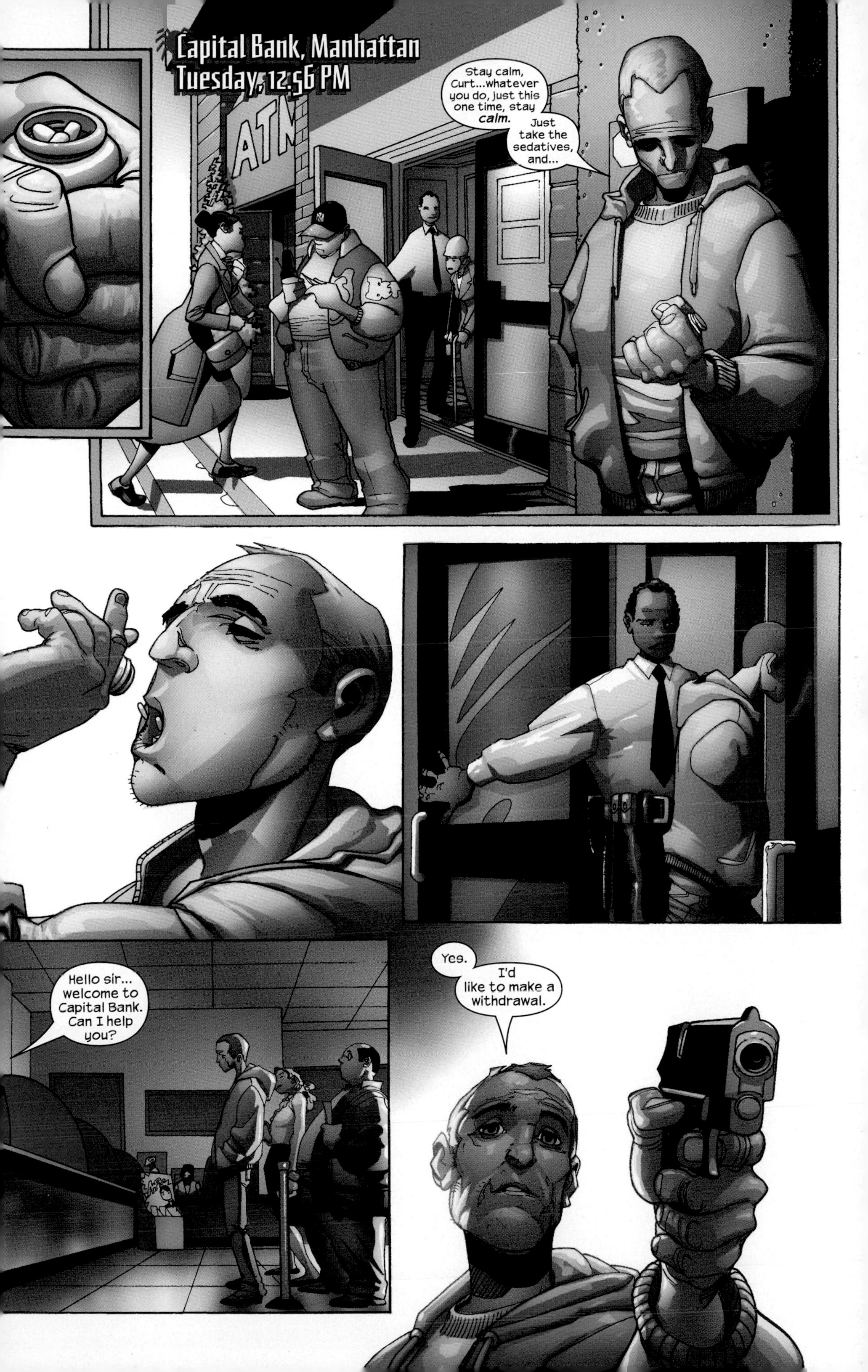
Capital Bank, Manhattan
Tuesday, 12:56 PM
Stay calm, Curt...whatever you do, just this one time, stay calm.
Just take the sedatives, and...
ATM
Hello sir... welcome to Capital Bank. Can I help you?
Yes.
I'd like to make a withdrawal.

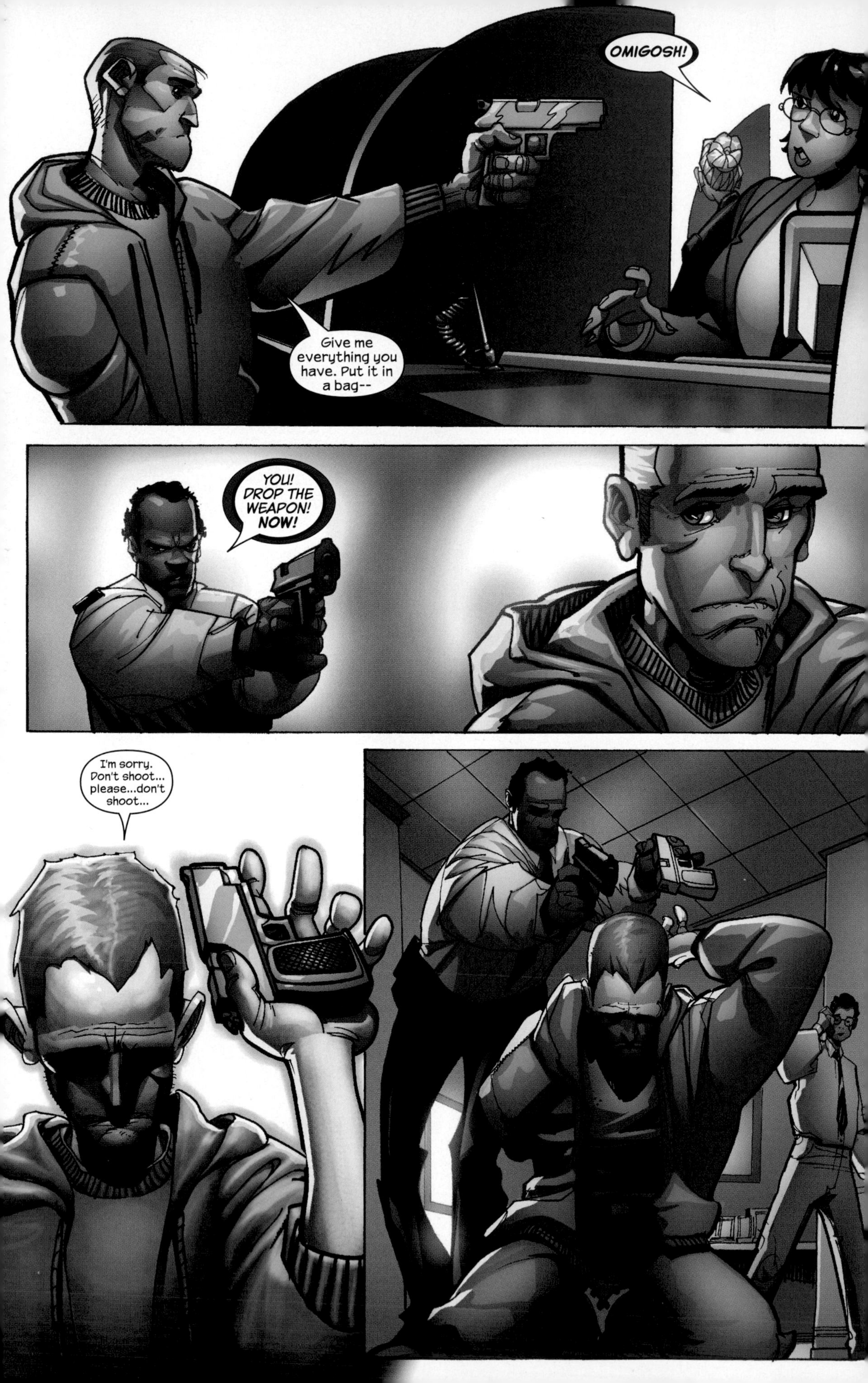
OMIGOSH!
Give me everything you have. Put it in a bag--
YOU! DROP THE WEAPON! NOW!
I'm sorry. Don't shoot... please...don't shoot...

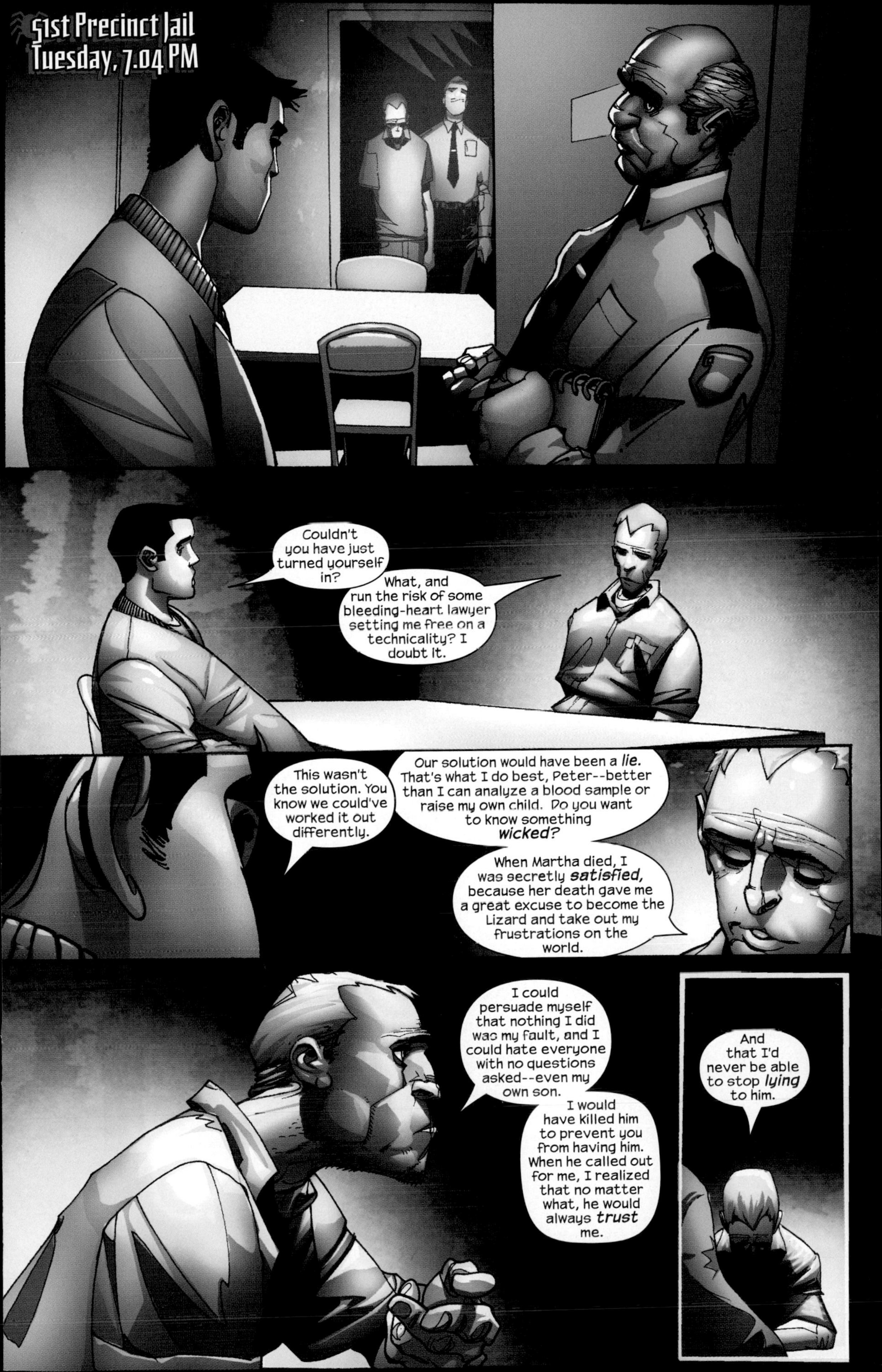
51st Precinct Jail
Tuesday, 7.04 PM
Couldn't you have just turned yourself in?
What, and run the risk of some bleeding-heart lawyer setting me free on a technicality? I doubt it.
This wasn't the solution. You know we could've worked it out differently.
Our solution would have been a *lie.* That's what I do best, Peter--better than I can analyze a blood sample or raise my own child. Do you want to know something ***wicked?***
When Martha died, I was secretly ***satisfied,*** because her death gave me a great excuse to become the Lizard and take out my frustrations on the world.
I could persuade myself that nothing I did was my fault, and I could hate everyone with no questions asked--even my own son.
I would have killed him to prevent you from having him. When he called out for me, I realized that no matter what, he would always ***trust*** me.
And that I'd never be able to stop *lying* to him.

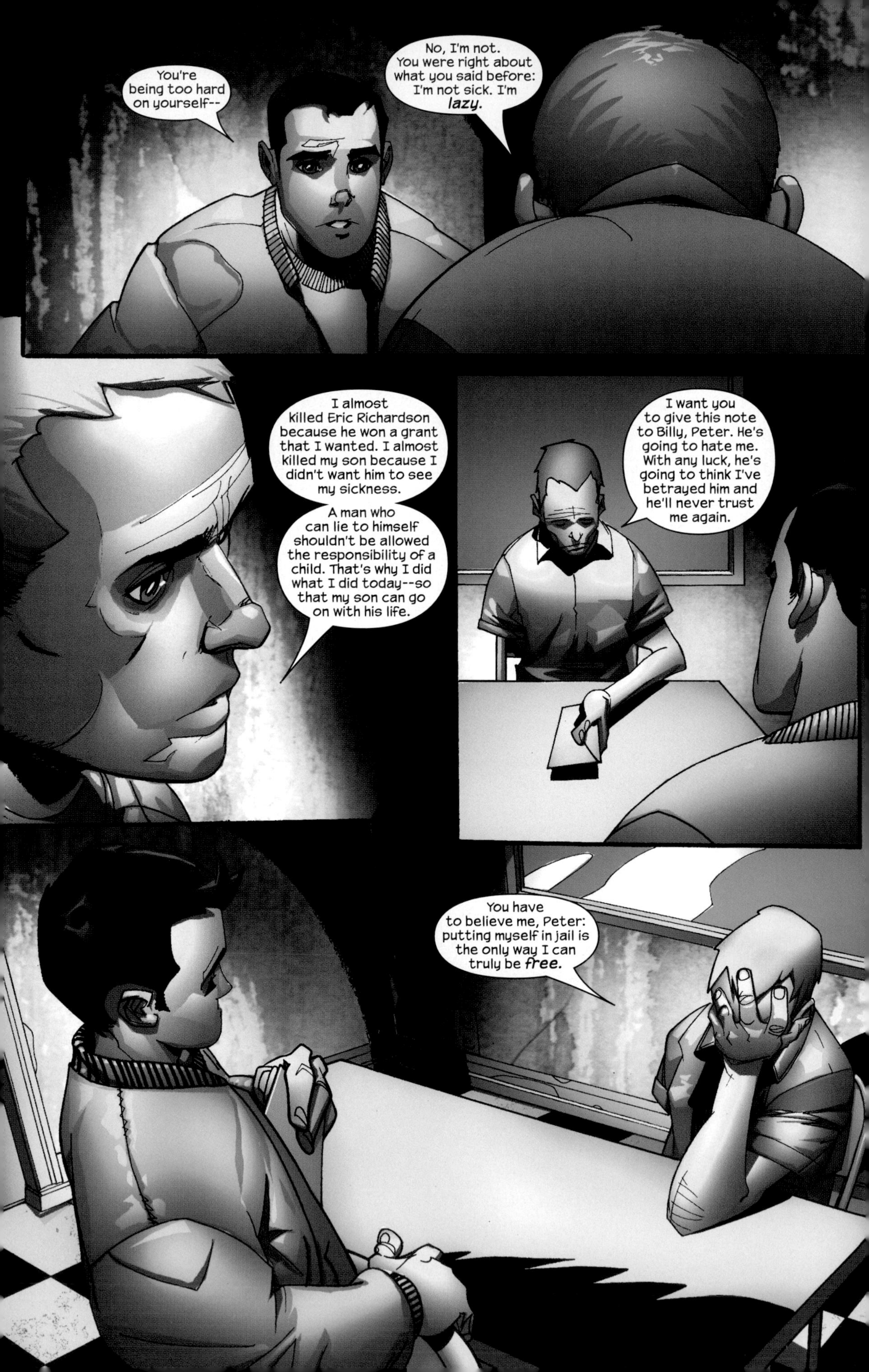
You're being too hard on yourself--
No, I'm not. You were right about what you said before: I'm not sick. I'm *lazy.*
I almost killed Eric Richardson because he won a grant that I wanted. I almost killed my son because I didn't want him to see my sickness.
A man who can lie to himself shouldn't be allowed the responsibility of a child. That's why I did what I did today--so that my son can go on with his life.
I want you to give this note to Billy, Peter. He's going to hate me. With any luck, he's going to think I've betrayed him and he'll never trust me again.
You have to believe me, Peter: putting myself in jail is the only way I can truly be *free.*

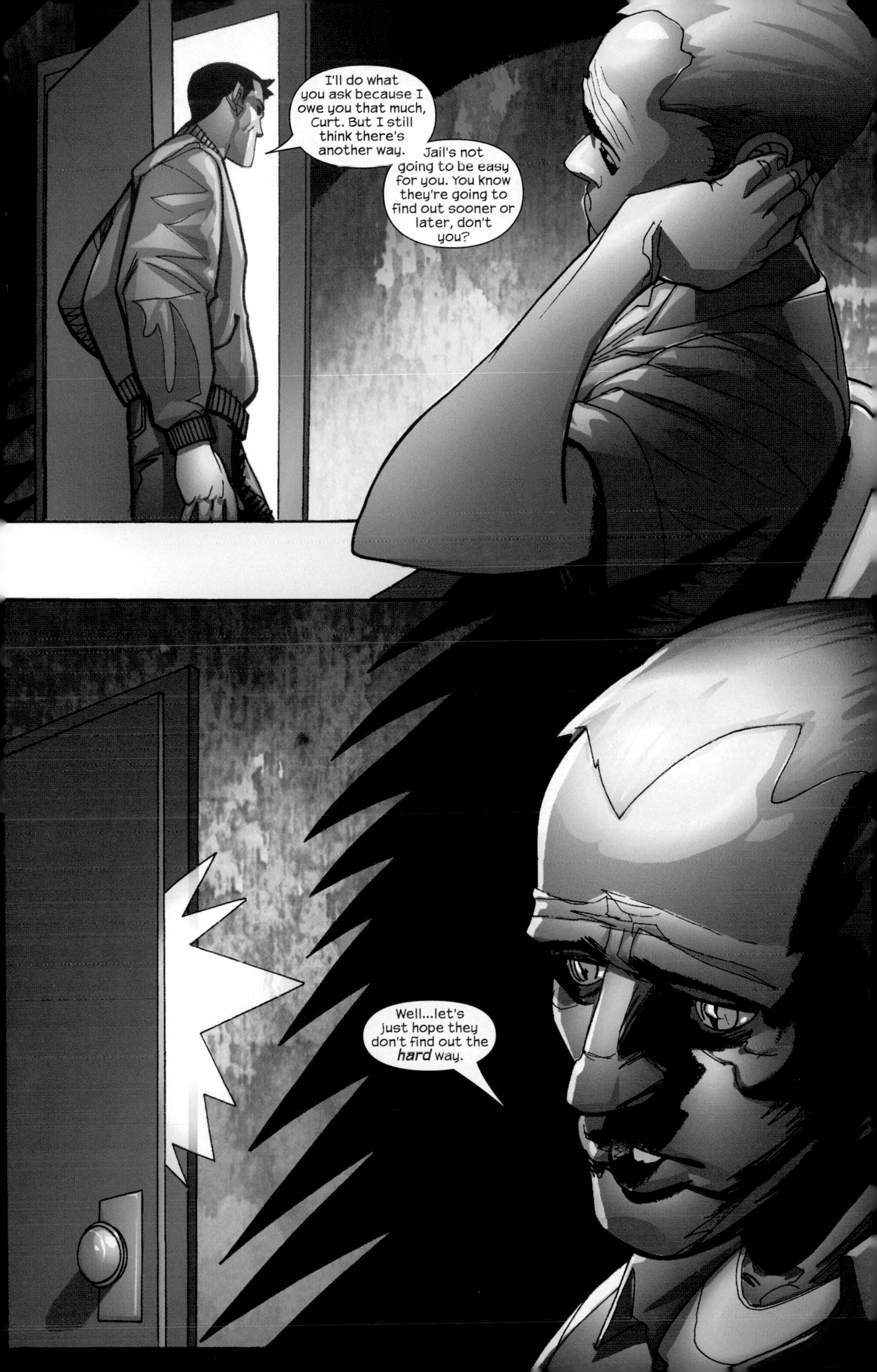
I'll do what you ask because I owe you that much, Curt. But I still think there's another way.
Jail's not going to be easy for you. You know they're going to find out sooner or later, don't you?
Well...let's just hope they don't find out the *hard* way.

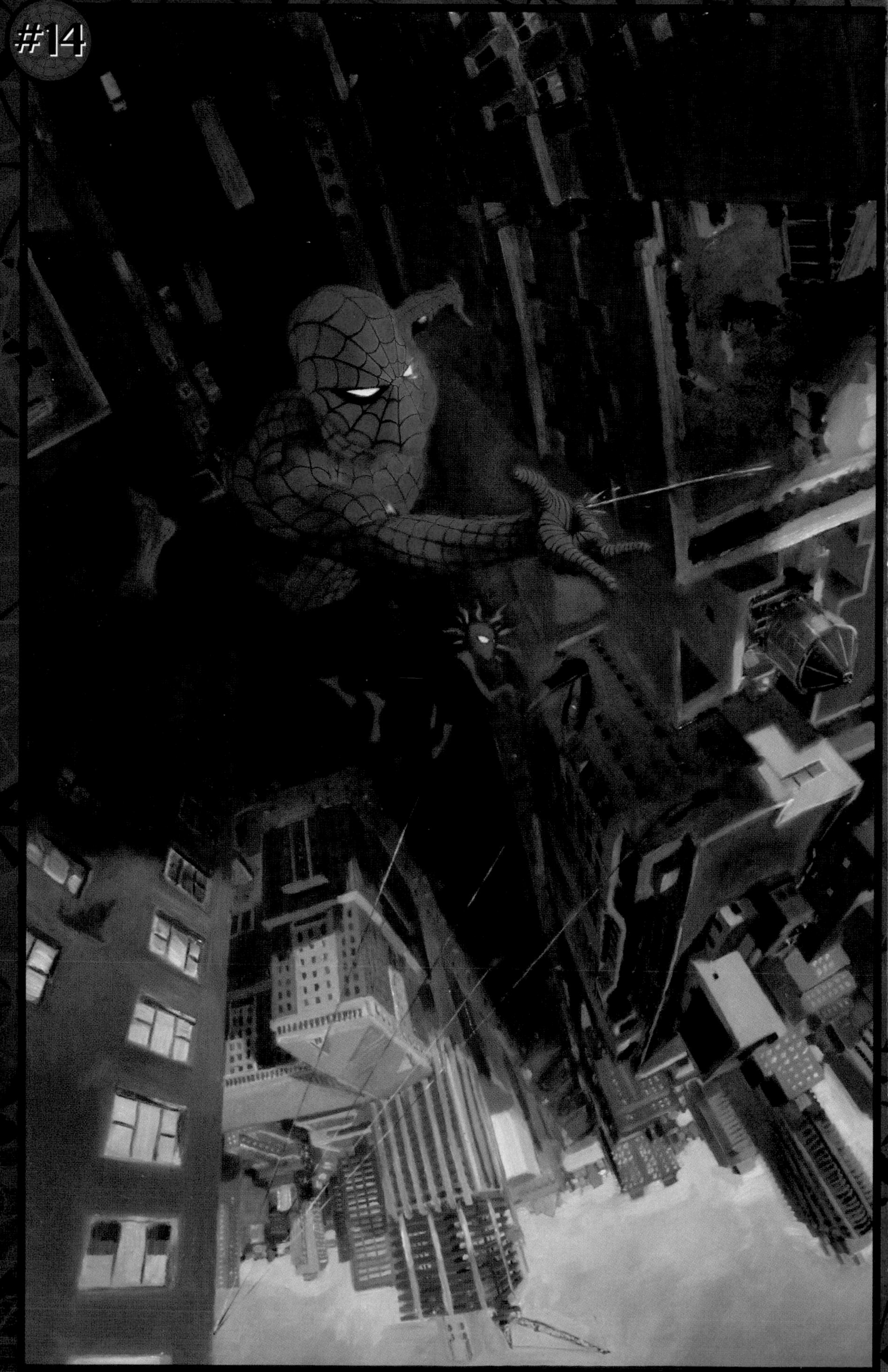
#14

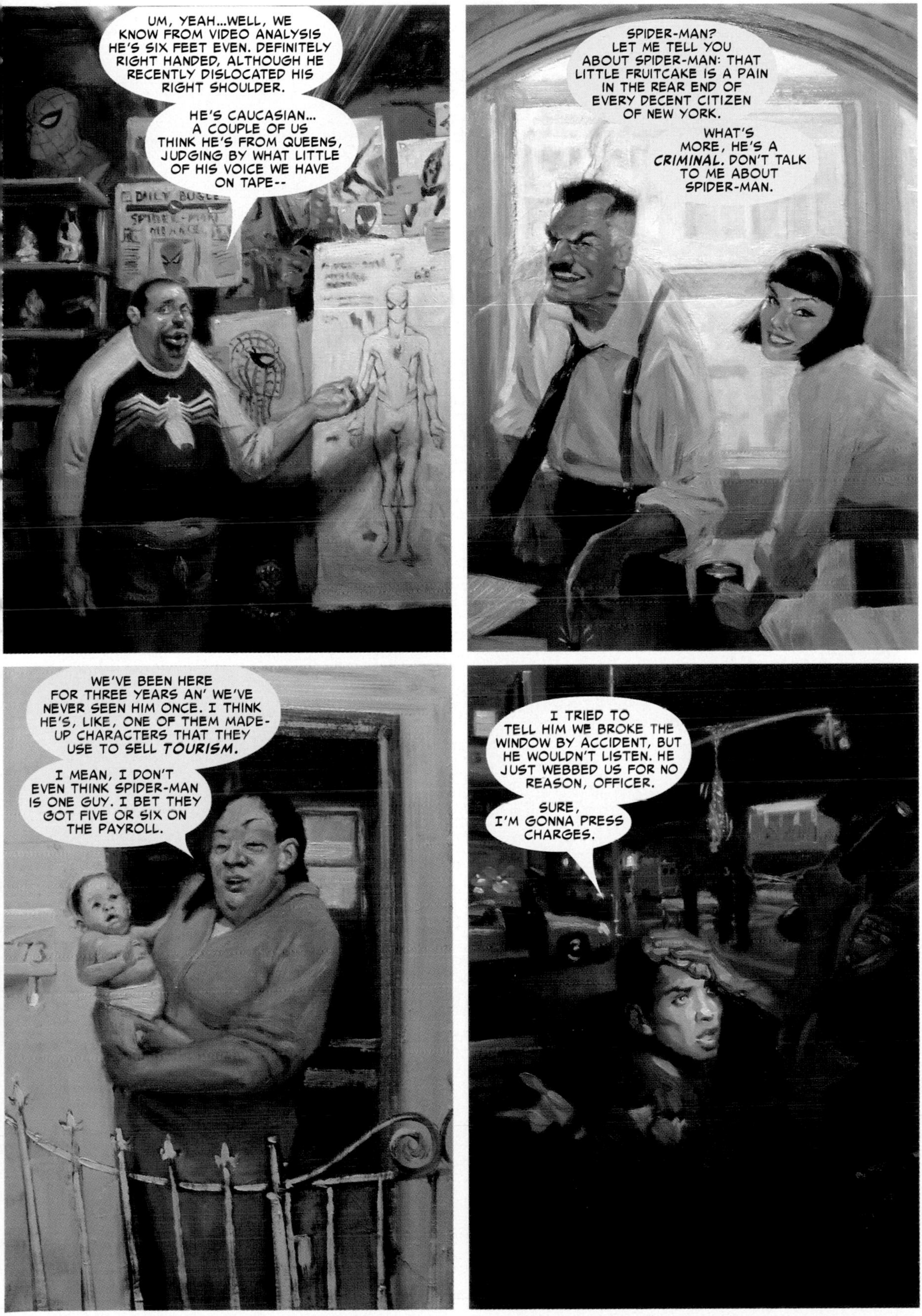
UM, YEAH...WELL, WE KNOW FROM VIDEO ANALYSIS HE'S SIX FEET EVEN. DEFINITELY RIGHT HANDED, ALTHOUGH HE RECENTLY DISLOCATED HIS RIGHT SHOULDER.
HE'S CAUCASIAN... A COUPLE OF US THINK HE'S FROM QUEENS, JUDGING BY WHAT LITTLE OF HIS VOICE WE HAVE ON TAPE--
DAILY BUGLE
SPIDER-MAN? LET ME TELL YOU ABOUT SPIDER-MAN: THAT LITTLE FRUITCAKE IS A PAIN IN THE REAR END OF EVERY DECENT CITIZEN OF NEW YORK.
WHAT'S MORE, HE'S A *CRIMINAL.* DON'T TALK TO ME ABOUT SPIDER-MAN.
WE'VE BEEN HERE FOR THREE YEARS AN' WE'VE NEVER SEEN HIM ONCE. I THINK HE'S, LIKE, ONE OF THEM MADE-UP CHARACTERS THAT THEY USE TO SELL *TOURISM.*
I MEAN, I DON'T EVEN THINK SPIDER-MAN IS ONE GUY. I BET THEY GOT FIVE OR SIX ON THE PAYROLL.
I TRIED TO TELL HIM WE BROKE THE WINDOW BY ACCIDENT, BUT HE WOULDN'T LISTEN. HE JUST WEBBED US FOR NO REASON, OFFICER.
SURE, I'M GONNA PRESS CHARGES.

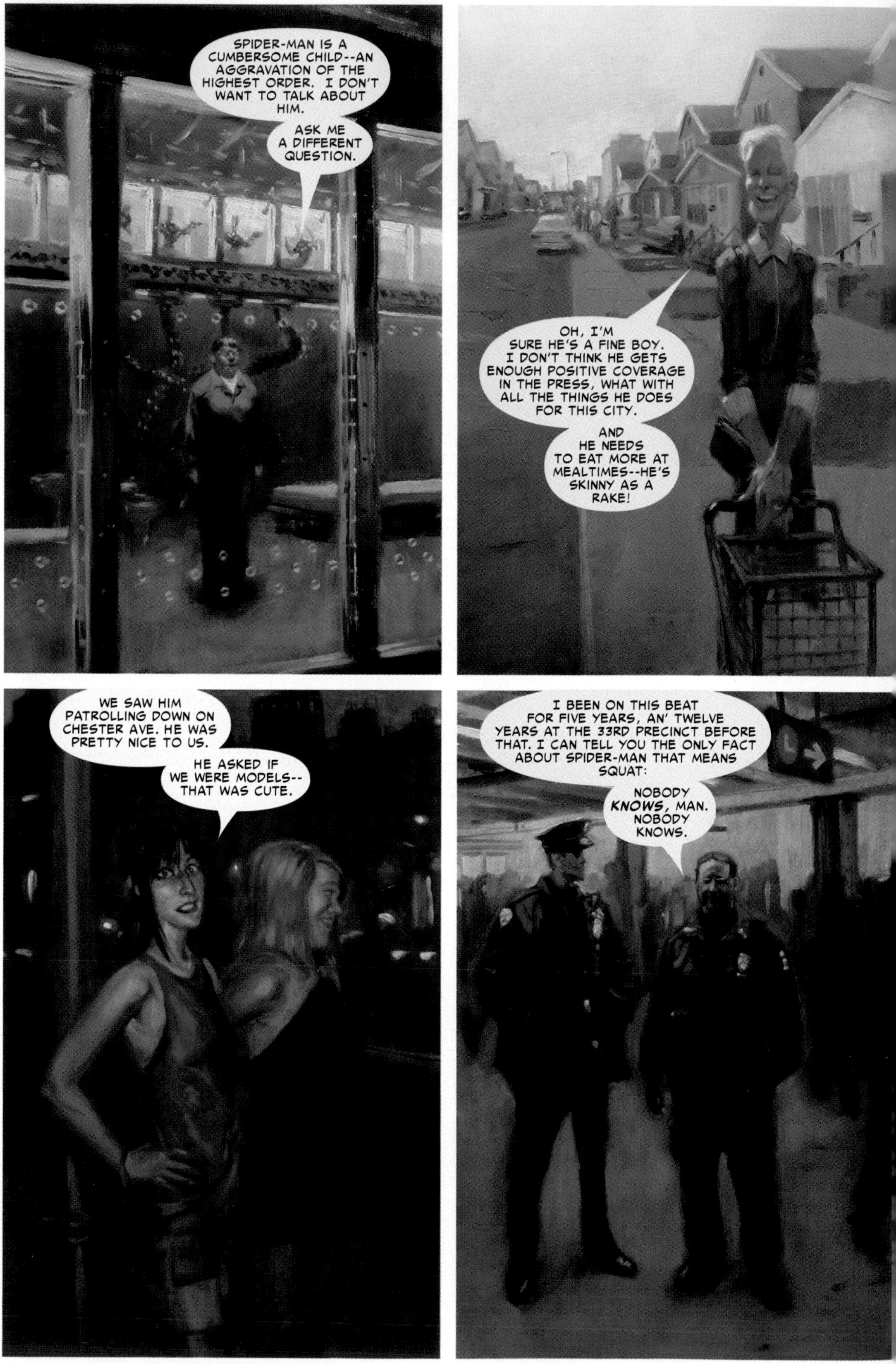
SPIDER-MAN IS A CUMBERSOME CHILD--AN AGGRAVATION OF THE HIGHEST ORDER. I DON'T WANT TO TALK ABOUT HIM.
ASK ME A DIFFERENT QUESTION.
OH, I'M SURE HE'S A FINE BOY. I DON'T THINK HE GETS ENOUGH POSITIVE COVERAGE IN THE PRESS, WHAT WITH ALL THE THINGS HE DOES FOR THIS CITY.
AND HE NEEDS TO EAT MORE AT MEALTIMES--HE'S SKINNY AS A RAKE!
WE SAW HIM PATROLLING DOWN ON CHESTER AVE. HE WAS PRETTY NICE TO US.
HE ASKED IF WE WERE MODELS--THAT WAS CUTE.
I BEEN ON THIS BEAT FOR FIVE YEARS, AN' TWELVE YEARS AT THE 33RD PRECINCT BEFORE THAT. I CAN TELL YOU THE ONLY FACT ABOUT SPIDER-MAN THAT MEANS SQUAT:
NOBODY *KNOWS*, MAN. NOBODY KNOWS.

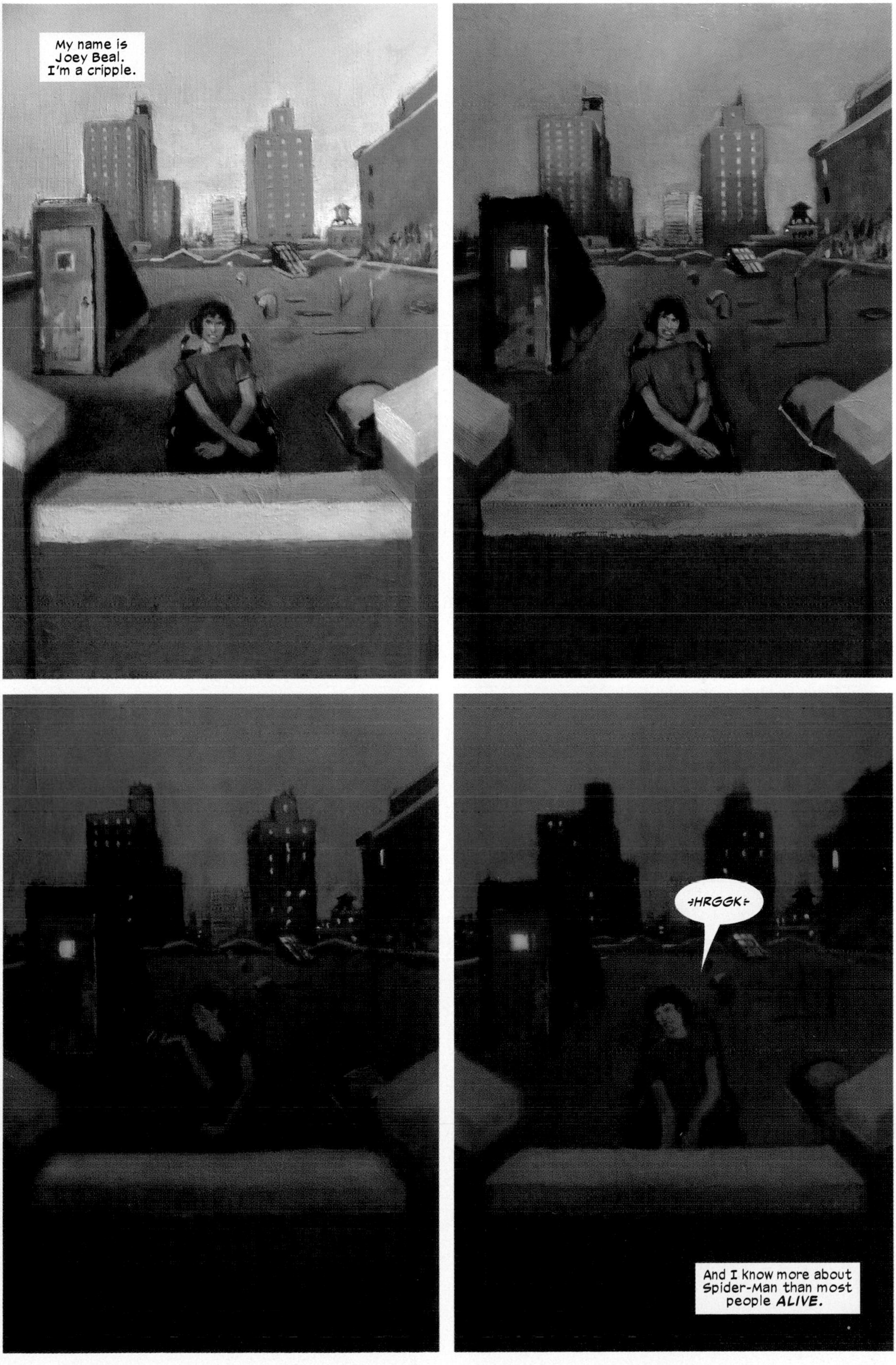
My name is Joey Beal. I'm a cripple.
HRGGK
And I know more about Spider-Man than most people ALIVE.

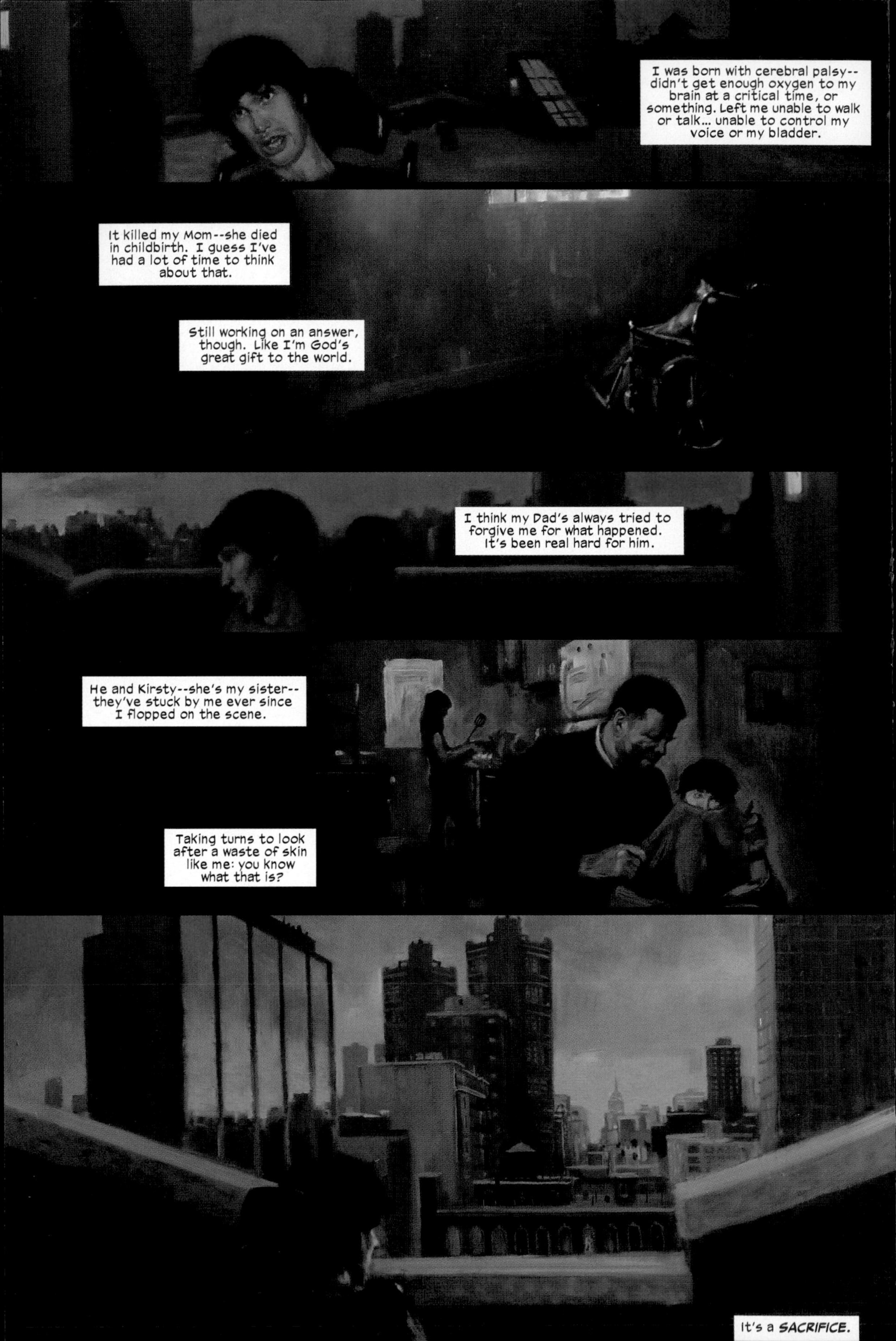
I was born with cerebral palsy--didn't get enough oxygen to my brain at a critical time, or something. Left me unable to walk or talk... unable to control my voice or my bladder.
It killed my Mom--she died in childbirth. I guess I've had a lot of time to think about that.
Still working on an answer, though. Like I'm God's great gift to the world.
I think my Dad's always tried to forgive me for what happened. It's been real hard for him.
He and Kirsty--she's my sister--they've stuck by me ever since I flopped on the scene.
Taking turns to look after a waste of skin like me: you know what that is?
It's a SACRIFICE.

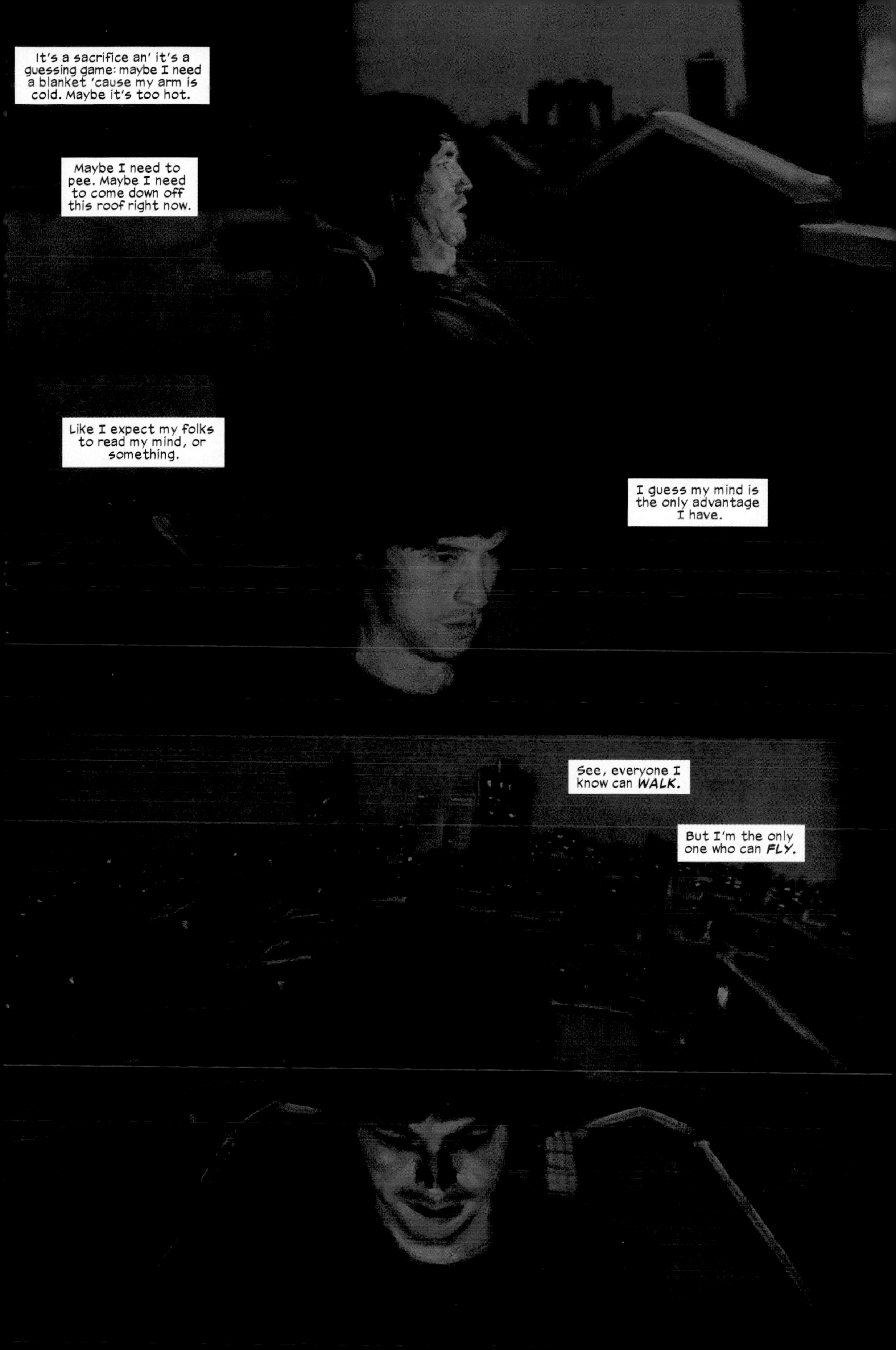
It's a sacrifice an' it's a guessing game: maybe I need a blanket 'cause my arm is cold. Maybe it's too hot.
Maybe I need to pee. Maybe I need to come down off this roof right now.
Like I expect my folks to read my mind, or something.
I guess my mind is the only advantage I have.
See, everyone I know can WALK.
But I'm the only one who can FLY.

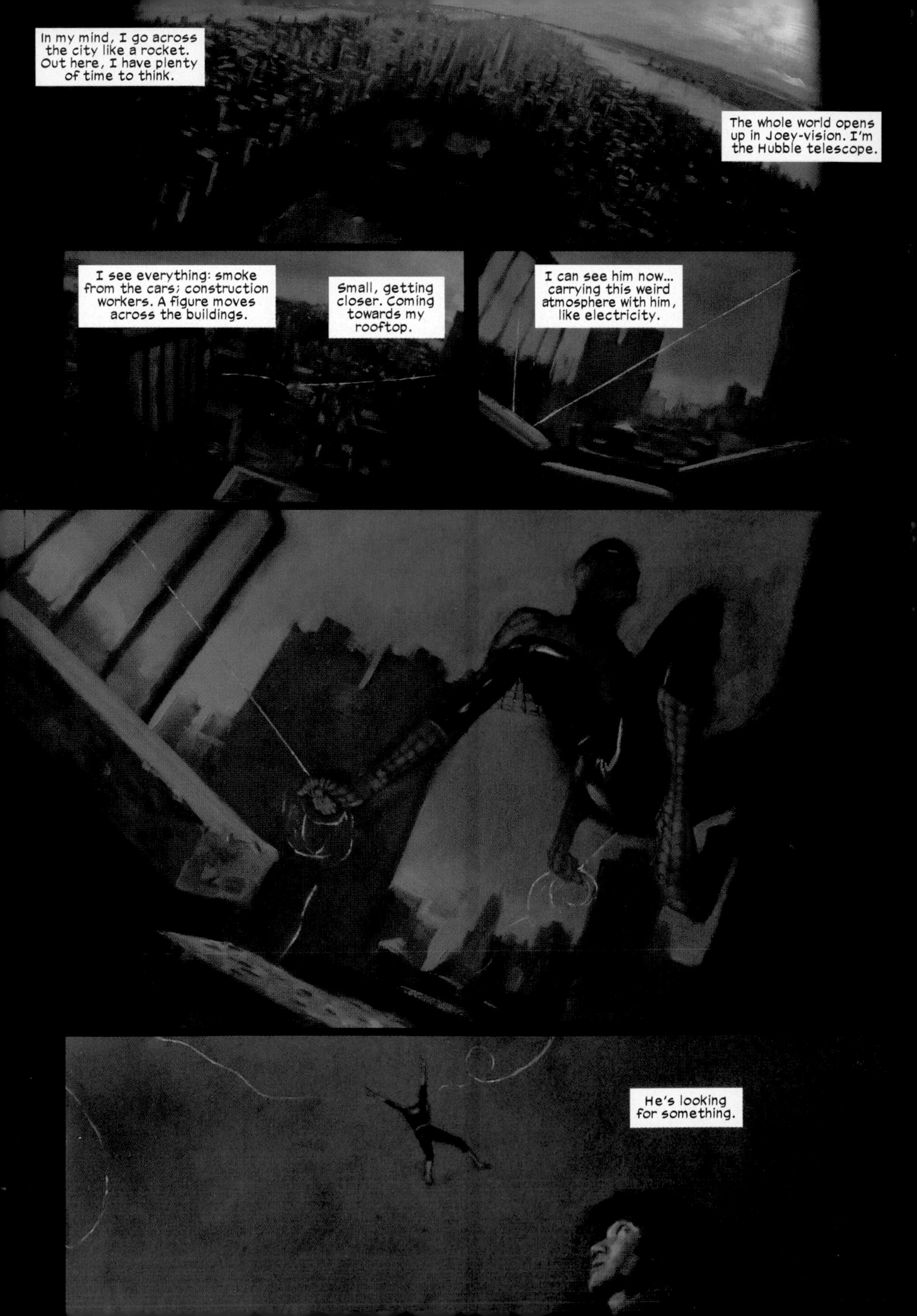
In my mind, I go across the city like a rocket. Out here, I have plenty of time to think.
The whole world opens up in Joey-vision. I'm the Hubble telescope.
I see everything: smoke from the cars; construction workers. A figure moves across the buildings.
Small, getting closer. Coming towards my rooftop.
I can see him now... carrying this weird atmosphere with him, like electricity.
He's looking for something.

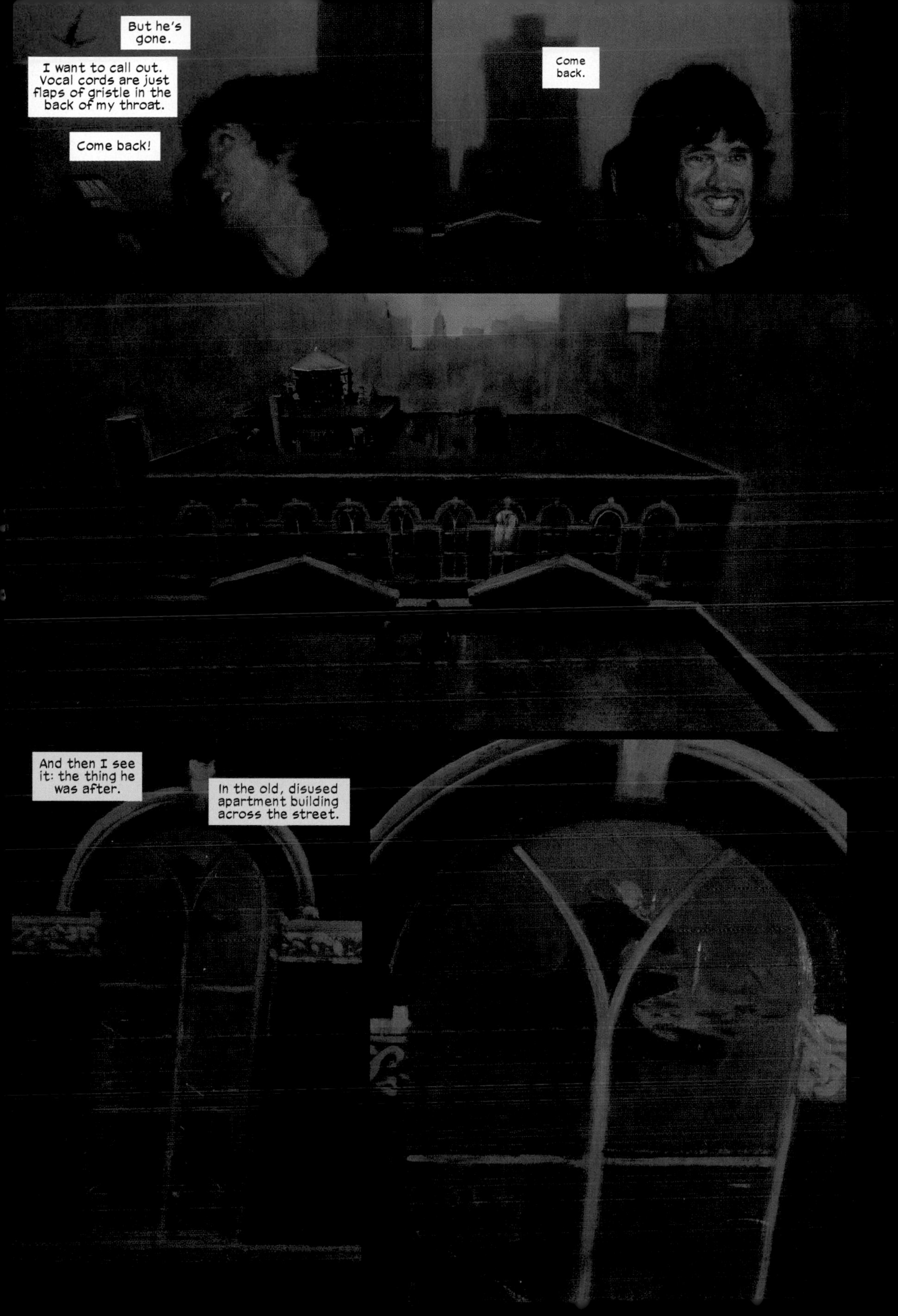
But he's gone.
I want to call out. Vocal cords are just flaps of gristle in the back of my throat.
Come back!
Come back.
And then I see it: the thing he was after.
In the old, disused apartment building across the street.

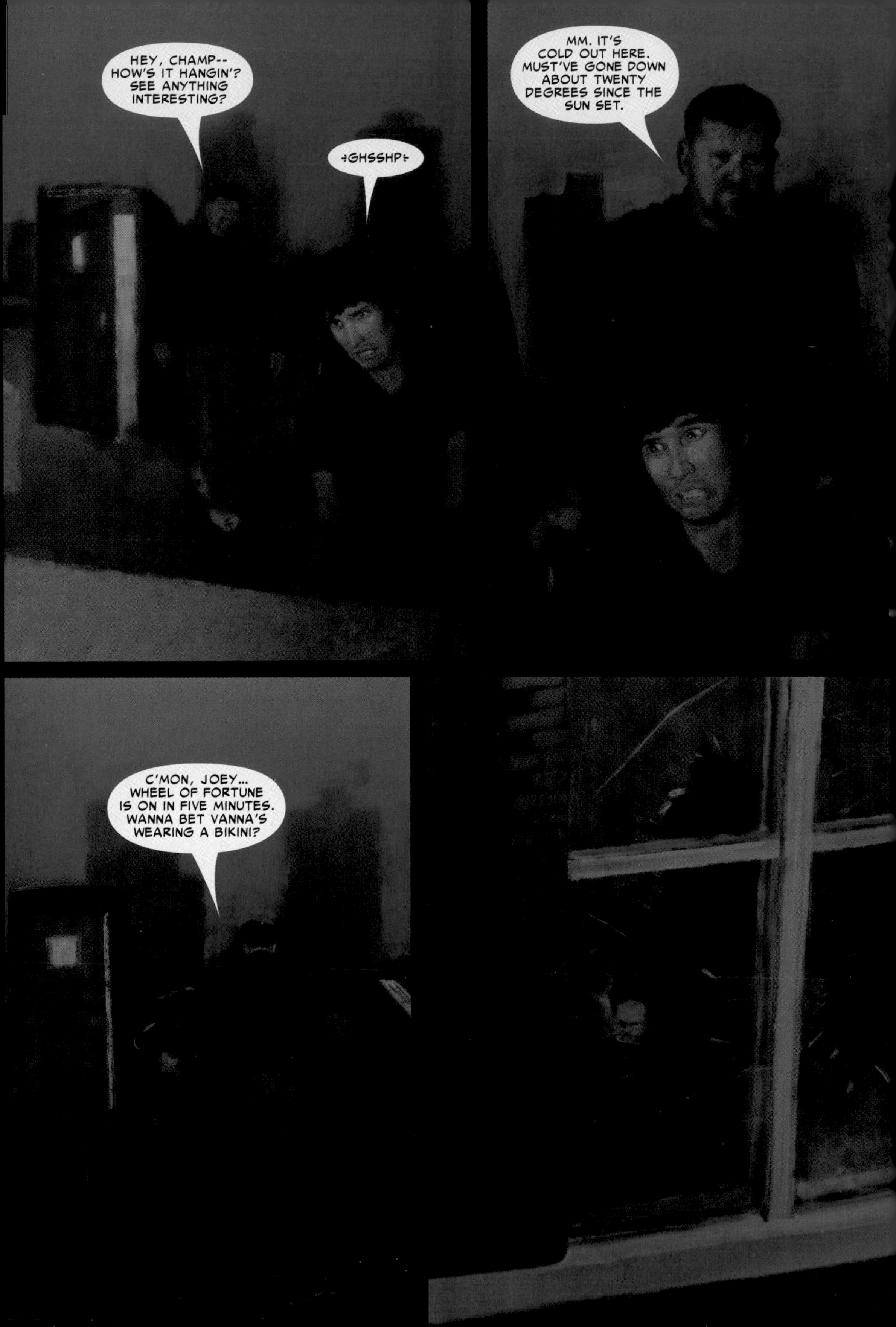
HEY, CHAMP-- HOW'S IT HANGIN'? SEE ANYTHING INTERESTING?
-GHSSHP-
MM. IT'S COLD OUT HERE. MUST'VE GONE DOWN ABOUT TWENTY DEGREES SINCE THE SUN SET.
C'MON, JOEY... WHEEL OF FORTUNE IS ON IN FIVE MINUTES. WANNA BET VANNA'S WEARING A BIKINI?

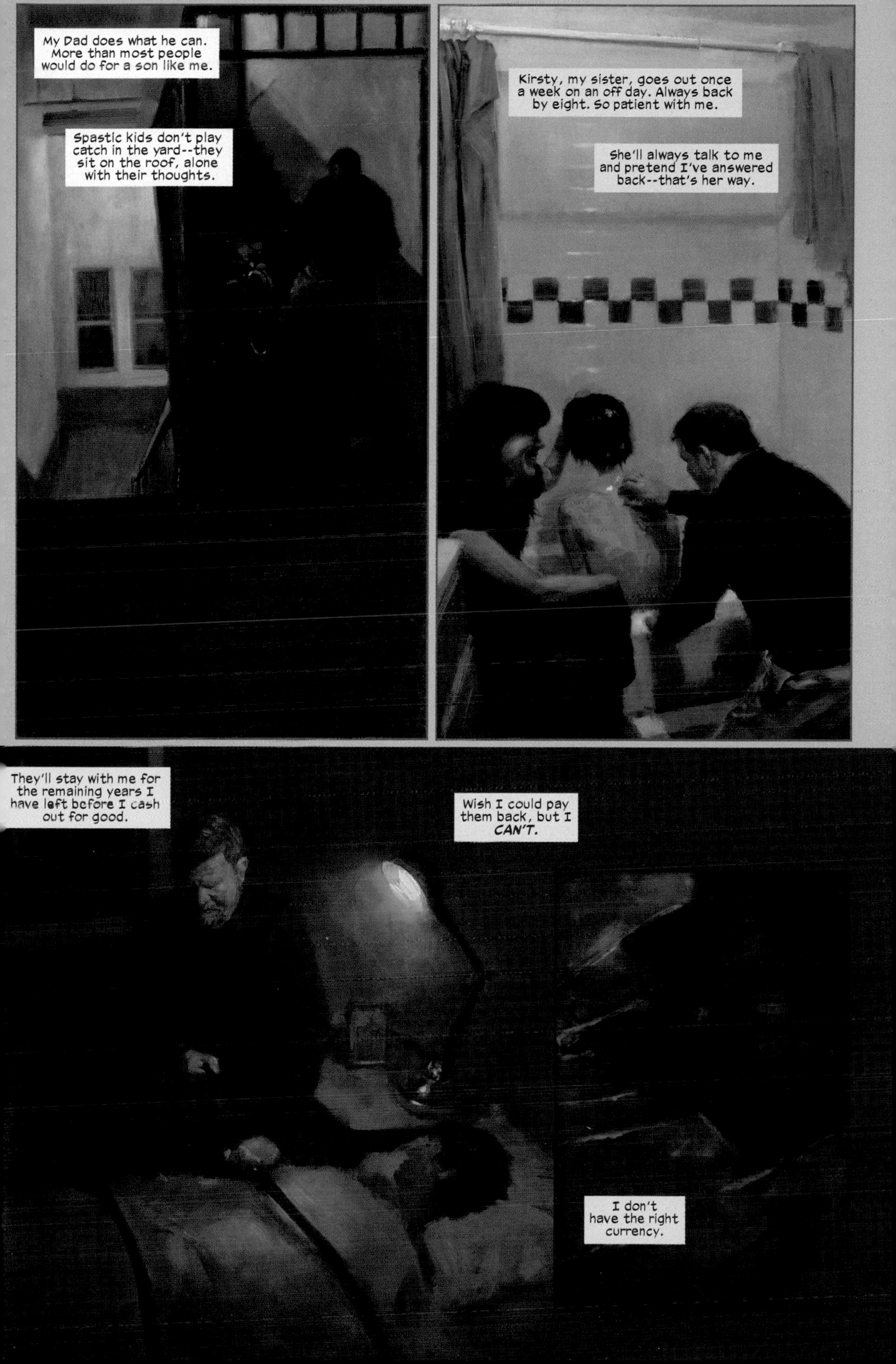
My Dad does what he can. More than most people would do for a son like me.
Spastic kids don't play catch in the yard--they sit on the roof, alone with their thoughts.
Kirsty, my sister, goes out once a week on an off day. Always back by eight. So patient with me.
She'll always talk to me and pretend I've answered back--that's her way.
They'll stay with me for the remaining years I have left before I cash out for good.
Wish I could pay them back, but I *CAN'T.*
I don't have the right currency.

HEY, DID YOU NOTICE ANYONE IN THAT OLD BUILDING ACROSS THE STREET, KIRST? I SWEAR THERE WAS SOMEONE OVER THERE LAST NIGHT.

MAYBE IT'S MAINTENANCE. I GOTTA GO, DAD-- I'M SEEING JOHN AT HIS GAME.

MAKE SURE YOU'RE BACK BY EIGHT. I HAVE A MEETING WITH A CLIENT.

WHAT ABOUT YOU, CHAMP? WHAT DO YOU WANT TO DO TODAY?

=NNRGH=

UPSTAIRS, HUH? OKAY, BUT I CAN'T COME BRING YOU DOWN UNTIL I GET BACK. I'LL MAKE SURE YOUR SISTER CHECKS IN FROM TIME TO TIME WHEN SHE GETS IN, 'KAY?

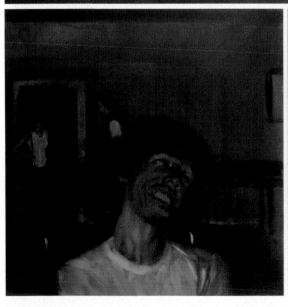

Wish I could tell them how I feel.

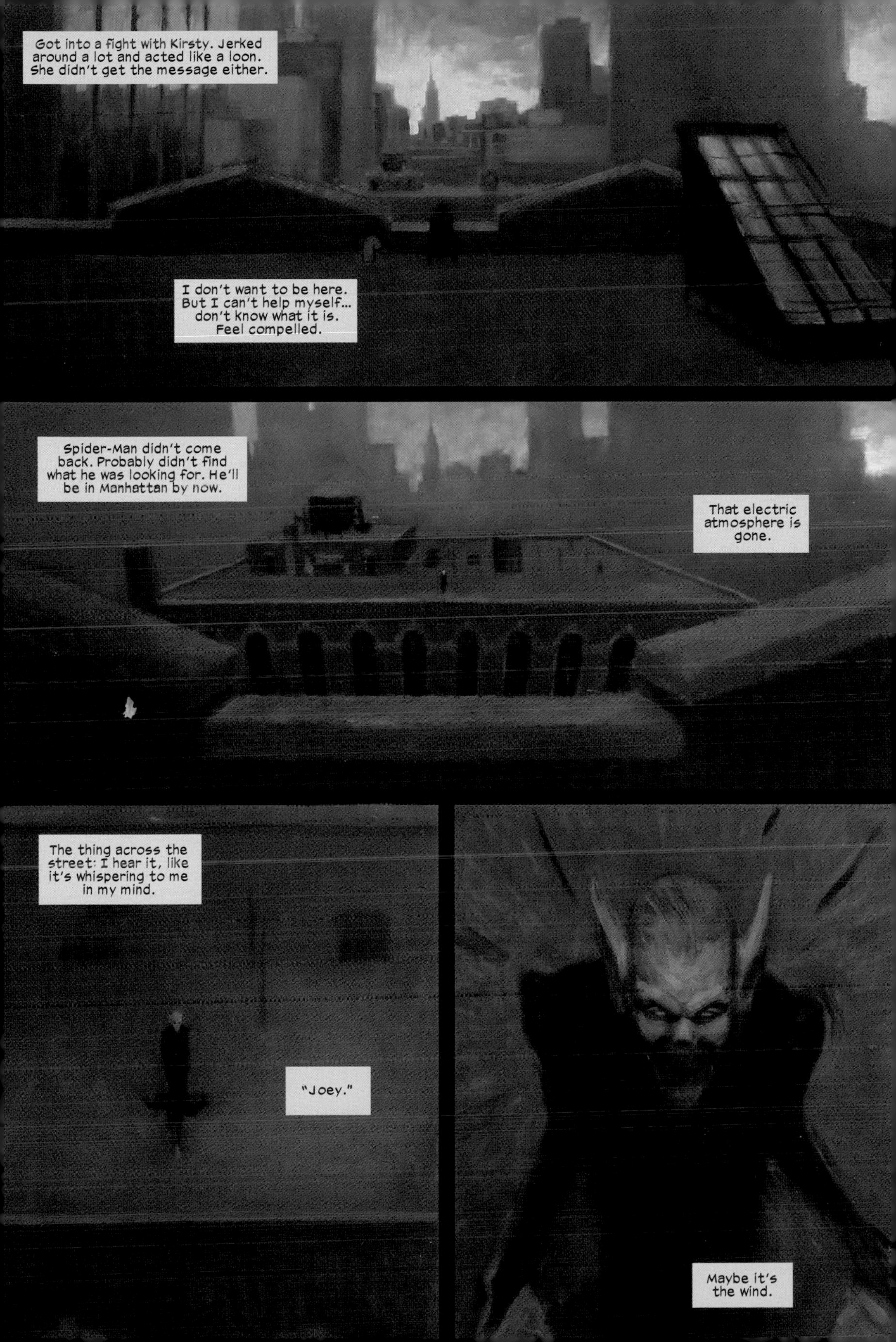
Got into a fight with Kirsty. Jerked around a lot and acted like a loon. She didn't get the message either.
I don't want to be here. But I can't help myself... don't know what it is. Feel compelled.
Spider-Man didn't come back. Probably didn't find what he was looking for. He'll be in Manhattan by now.
That electric atmosphere is gone.
The thing across the street: I hear it, like it's whispering to me in my mind.
"Joey."
Maybe it's the wind.

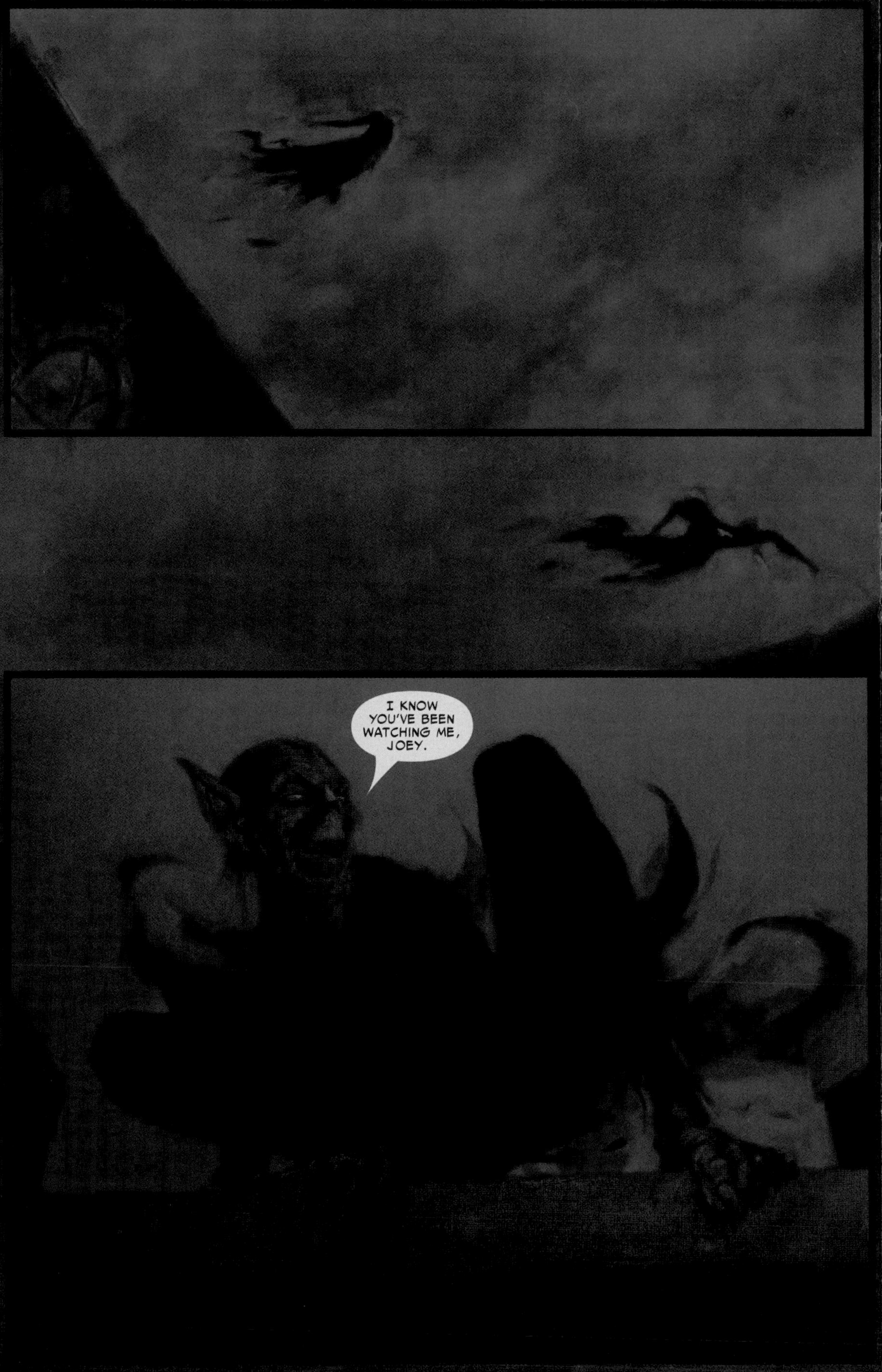
I KNOW YOU'VE BEEN WATCHING ME, JOEY.

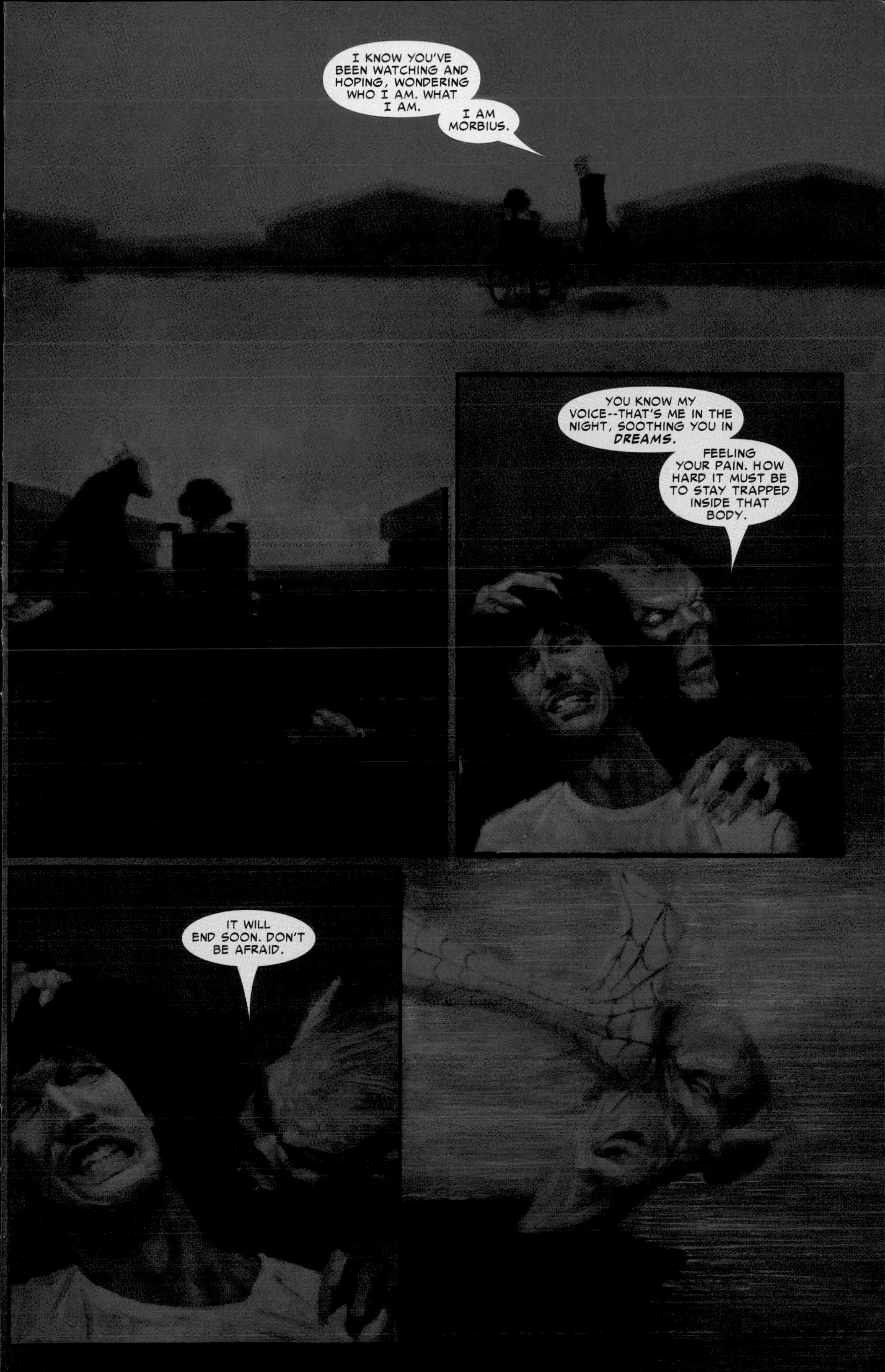
I KNOW YOU'VE BEEN WATCHING AND HOPING, WONDERING WHO I AM. WHAT I AM.
I AM MORBIUS.
YOU KNOW MY VOICE--THAT'S ME IN THE NIGHT, SOOTHING YOU IN DREAMS.
FEELING YOUR PAIN. HOW HARD IT MUST BE TO STAY TRAPPED INSIDE THAT BODY.
IT WILL END SOON. DON'T BE AFRAID.

YEEHAW! SPIDER-BOMBS AT TEN O'CLOCK!
DUDE, YOU NEED TO PICK ON SOMEONE YOUR OWN SIZE, SPECIES AND/OR GENDER.
SAY, WHAT GENDER ARE YOU, ANYWAY?
SPIDER-MAN!
THAT'S MY NAME. DON'T WEAR IT--
--OOP.

AND NOW, LIVE FROM BROOKLYN, THE AMAZING LIVING VAMPIRE--DRACULA-LITE!
MARVEL AT HIS GIRLISH FIGURE! SWOON OVER HIS FASHIONABLE CLOTHING AND SHI TZU-LIKE OVERBITE!
THIS WAS NOT YOUR TIME, SPIDER-MAN. NOT YOUR AFFAIR.
I WILL KILL YOU NOW FOR WHAT YOU HAVE DONE.
BRING IT ON, TOOTH BOY.

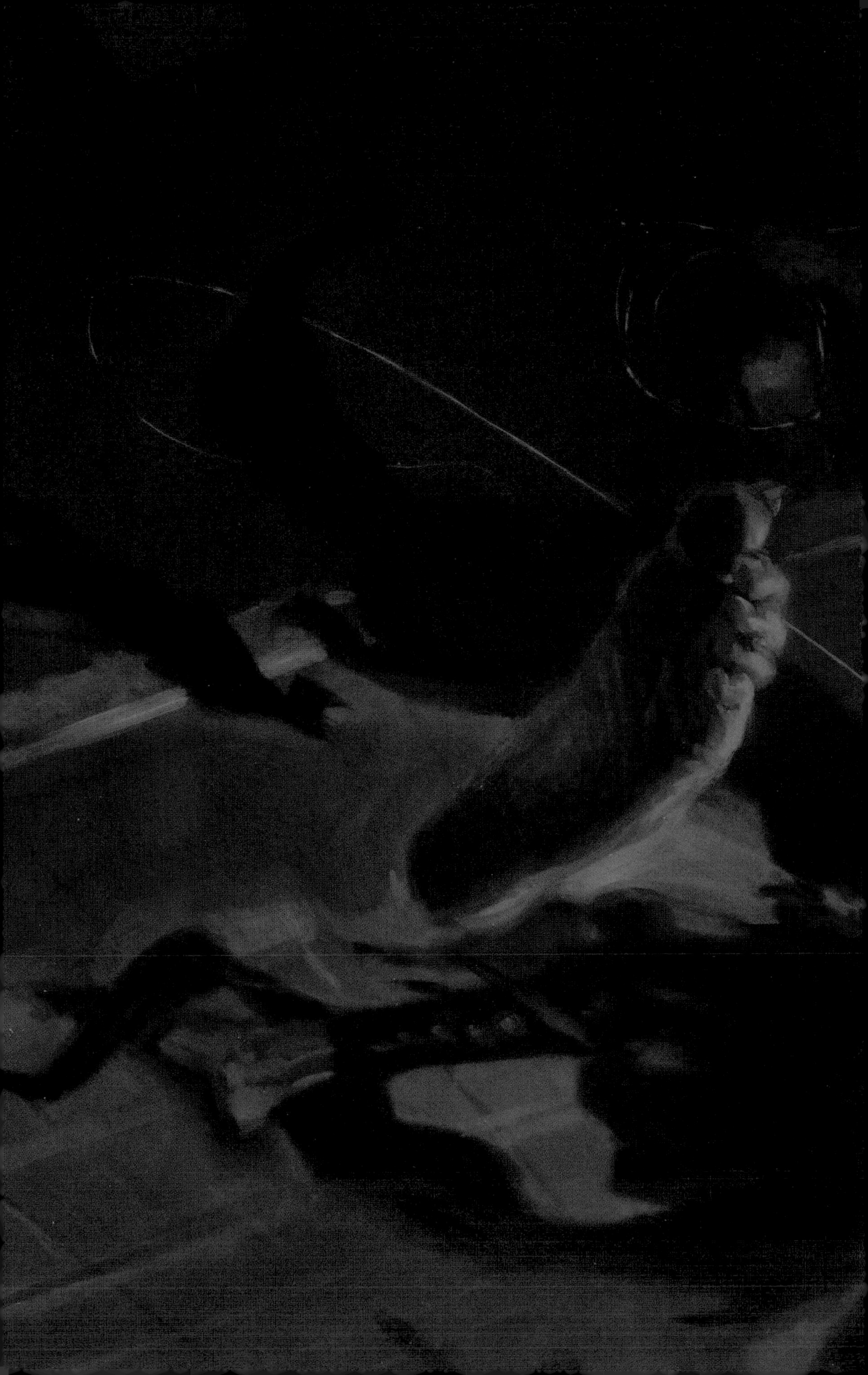

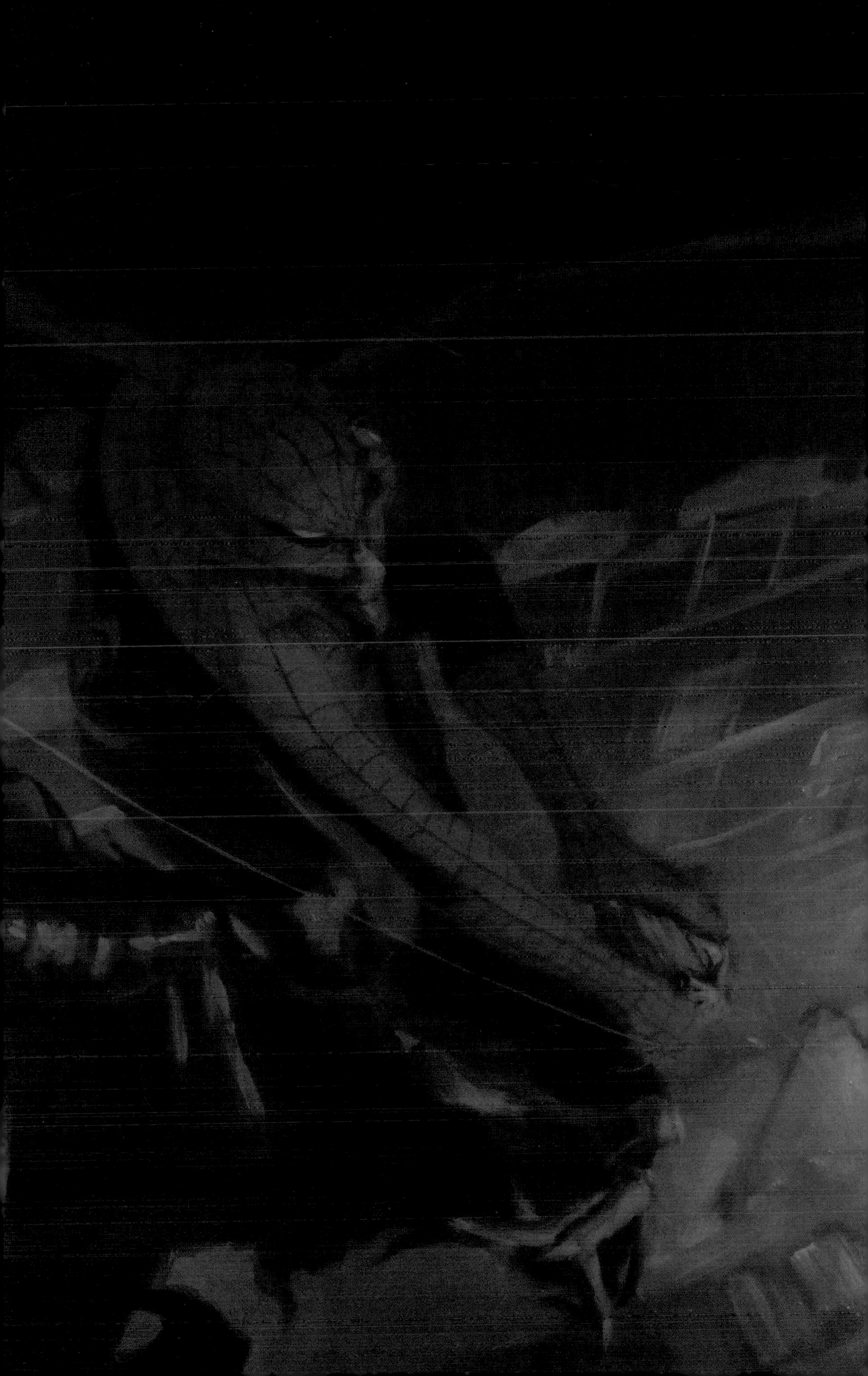

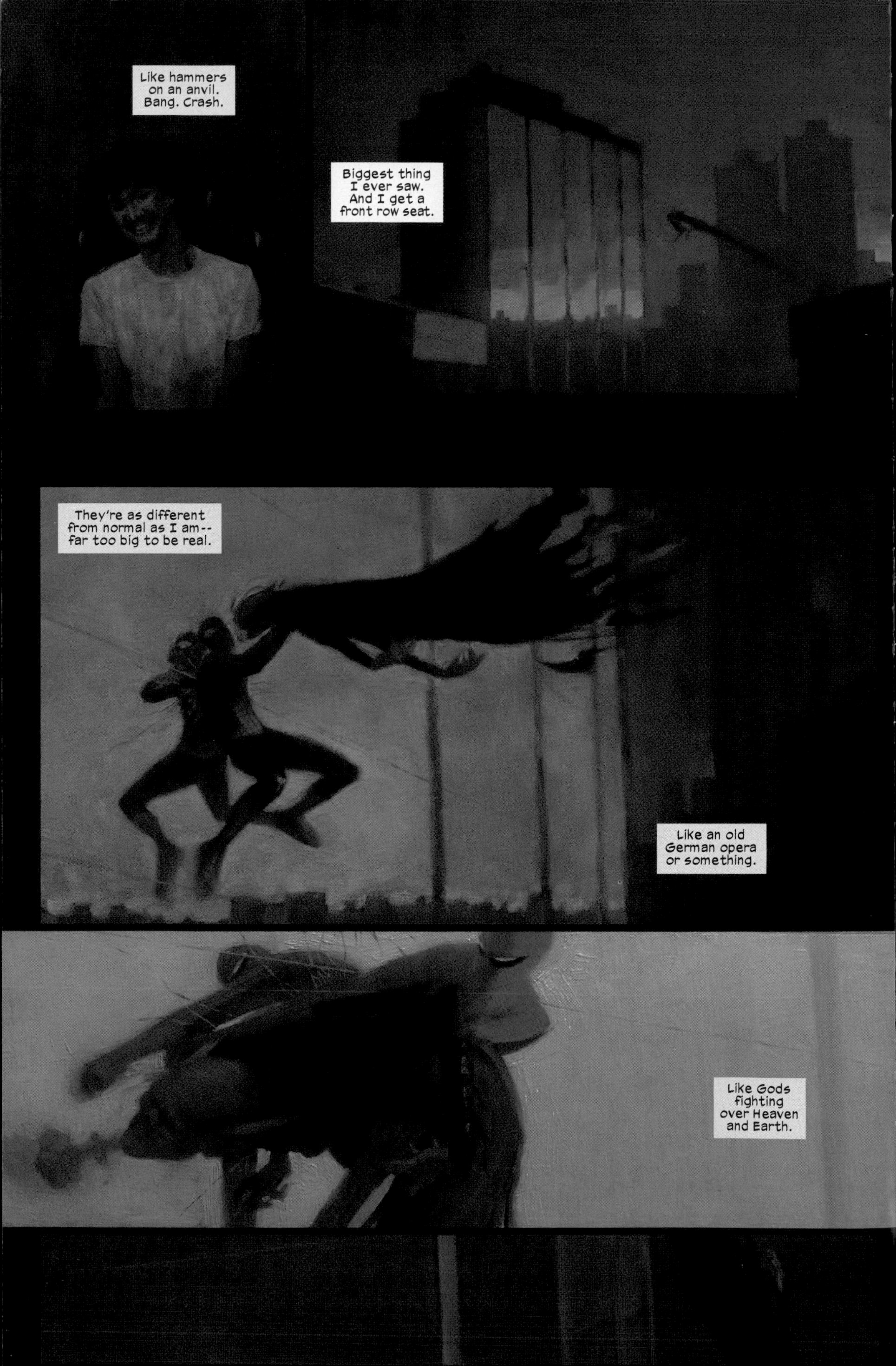
Like hammers on an anvil. Bang. Crash.
Biggest thing I ever saw. And I get a front row seat.
They're as different from normal as I am-- far too big to be real.
Like an old German opera or something.
Like Gods fighting over Heaven and Earth.

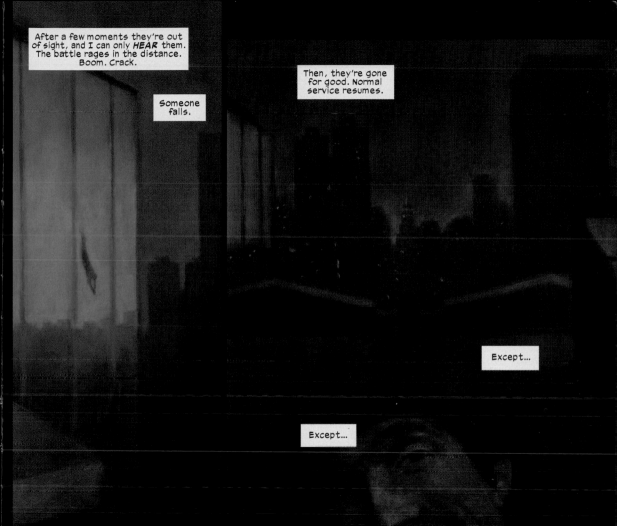

After a few moments they're out of sight, and I can only *HEAR* them. The battle rages in the distance. Boom. Crack.

Someone falls.

Then, they're gone for good. Normal service resumes.

Except...

Except...

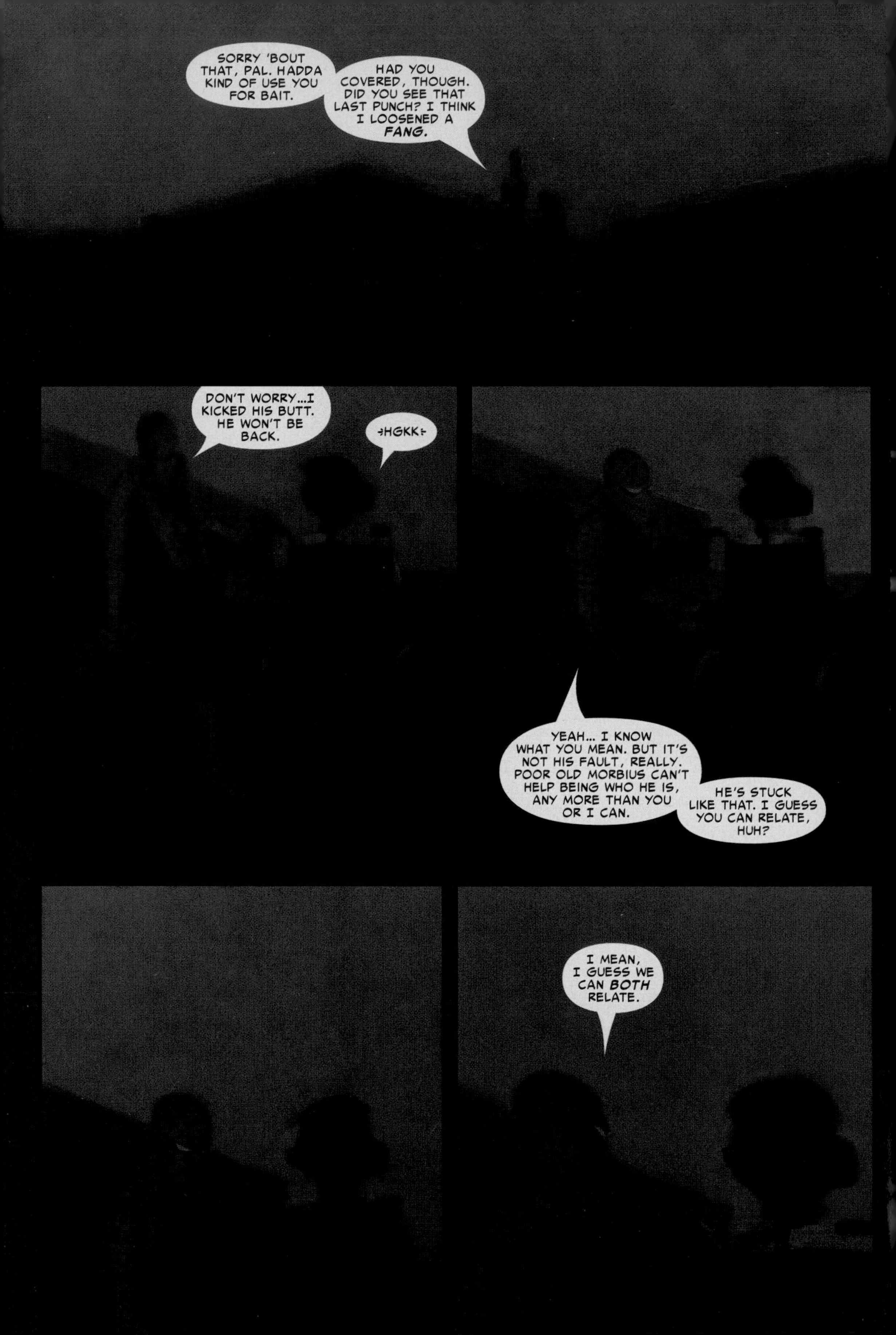
SORRY 'BOUT THAT, PAL. HADDA KIND OF USE YOU FOR BAIT.
HAD YOU COVERED, THOUGH. DID YOU SEE THAT LAST PUNCH? I THINK I LOOSENED A *FANG.*
DON'T WORRY...I KICKED HIS BUTT. HE WON'T BE BACK.
HGKK
YEAH... I KNOW WHAT YOU MEAN. BUT IT'S NOT HIS FAULT, REALLY. POOR OLD MORBIUS CAN'T HELP BEING WHO HE IS, ANY MORE THAN YOU OR I CAN.
HE'S STUCK LIKE THAT. I GUESS YOU CAN RELATE, HUH?
I MEAN, I GUESS WE CAN *BOTH* RELATE.

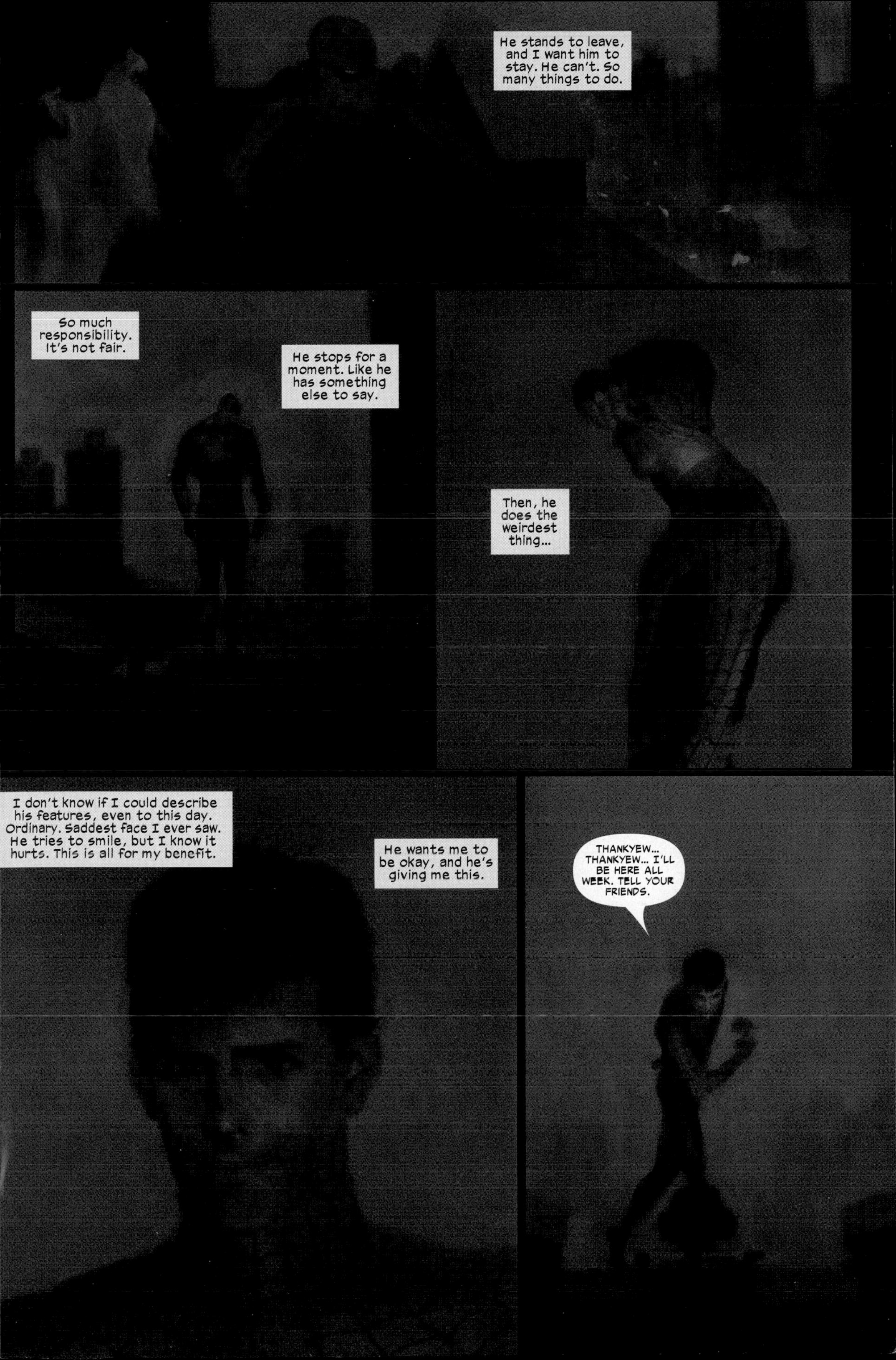
He stands to leave, and I want him to stay. He can't. So many things to do.
So much responsibility. It's not fair.
He stops for a moment. Like he has something else to say.
Then, he does the weirdest thing...
I don't know if I could describe his features, even to this day. Ordinary. Saddest face I ever saw. He tries to smile, but I know it hurts. This is all for my benefit.
He wants me to be okay, and he's giving me this.
THANKYEW... THANKYEW... I'LL BE HERE ALL WEEK. TELL YOUR FRIENDS.

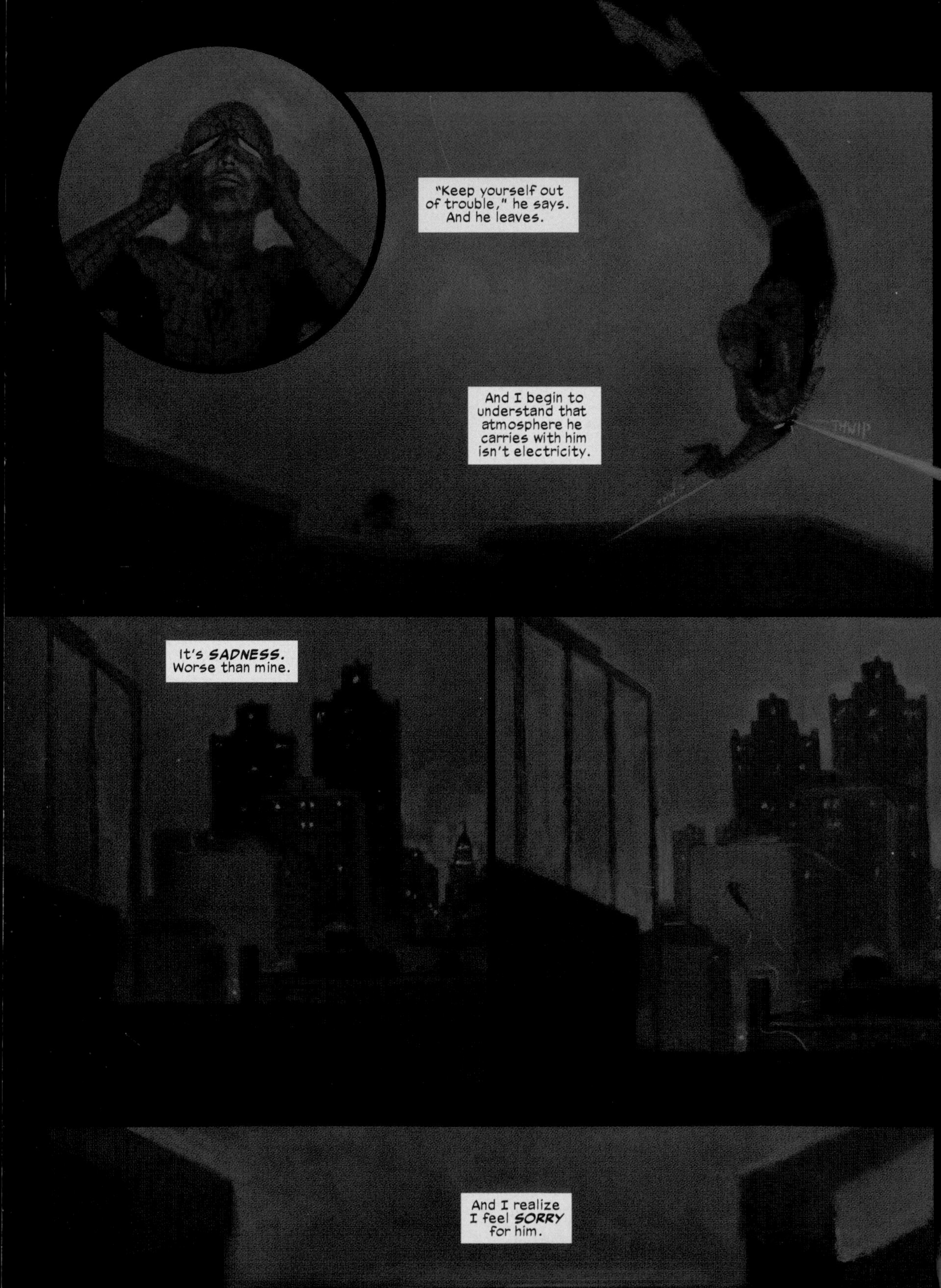
"Keep yourself out of trouble," he says. And he leaves.
And I begin to understand that atmosphere he carries with him isn't electricity.
THWIP
It's **SADNESS.** Worse than mine.
And I realize I feel **SORRY** for him.

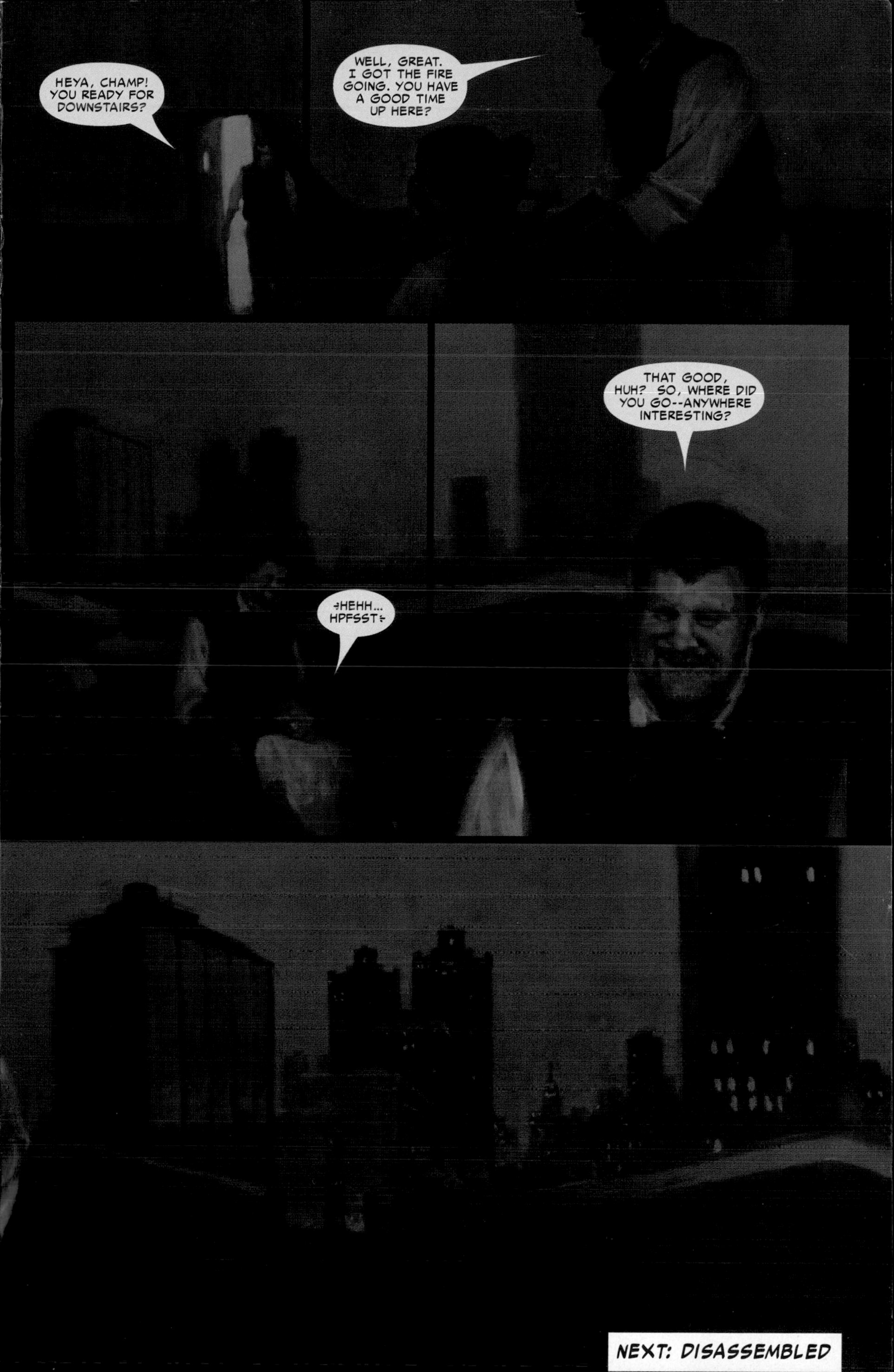
HEYA, CHAMP! YOU READY FOR DOWNSTAIRS?
WELL, GREAT. I GOT THE FIRE GOING. YOU HAVE A GOOD TIME UP HERE?
THAT GOOD, HUH? SO, WHERE DID YOU GO--ANYWHERE INTERESTING?
=HEHH... HPFSST=
NEXT: DISASSEMBLED

Paolo Rivera Sketchbook

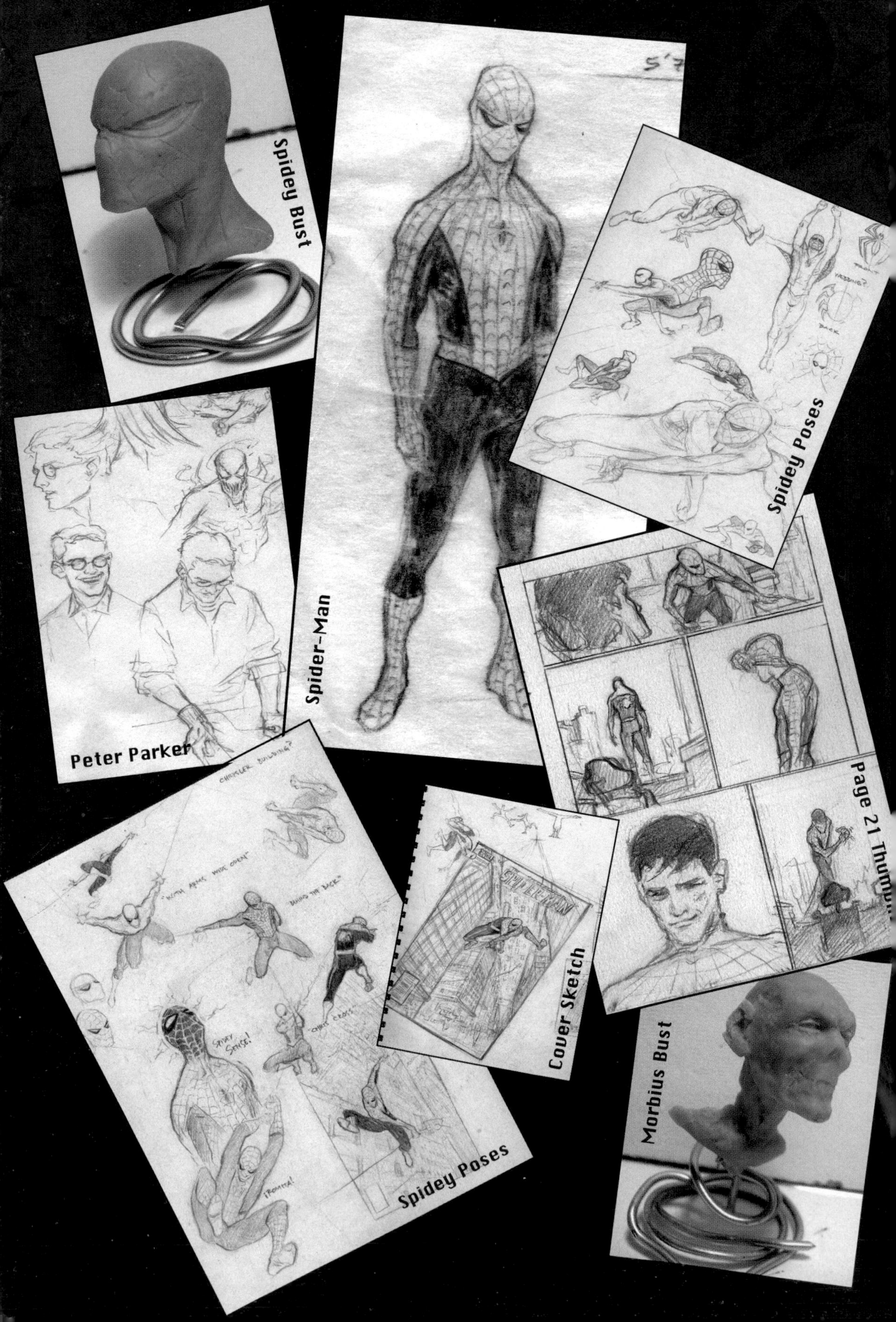

Spidey Bust
Spider-Man
Spidey Poses
Peter Parker
Page 21 Thumb...
Spidey Poses
Cover Sketch
Morbius Bust